SCHOOL ATLAS 1924

BY

J.G. BARTHOLOMEW

WITH AN INTRODUCTION BY

L.W. LYDE M.A.

PROFESSOR OF ECONOMIC GEOGRAPHY, UNIVERSITY OF LONDON

OLD HOUSE BOOKS
MORETONHAMPSTEAD DEVON
WWW.OldHouseBooks.co.uk

First Published as The Oxford Economic Atlas which became a bestselling school text book before the second world war. It has now been reissued by Old House Books.

Old House Books produce facsimile copies of long out of print maps and books that we believe deserve a second innings. Our reprints are of interest to genealogists and local historians. Other titles have been chosen to explore the character of life in years gone by and are helpful to anyone who wishes to know a bit more about the lives of their ancestors, or the area in which they live.

For details of other Old House Books titles please visit our website www.OldHouseBooks.co.uk or request a catalogue.

First Published by Oxford University Press in 1924
This edition was published in 2008 by
© Old House Books
The Old Police Station, Pound Street, Moretonhampstead,
Devon TQ13 8PA UK
Tel: 01647 440707 Fax: 01647 440202
info@OldHouseBooks.co.uk www.OldHouseBooks.co.uk
ISBN 978 1 873590 72 0

Printed in India

INTRODUCTION

School Geography must practically be limited to a study of the Earth only in relation to man; and, even with this limitation, there is a wealth of material available that is far beyond the needs or possibilities of any ordinary School course. The selection of material out of this superabundance runs generally on one of three lines—political, historic, or economic; and, of the three, the last is concerned with the material that is of most use to the average boy in his subsequent career. In each case the educational end is the same—the training of the imagination, so that it may be able to picture truly distant lands and foreign peoples; and in each case the treatment is identical except for a slight difference in the choice of details. Under these circumstances there is, naturally, a tendency to select such details for a School course from that side of the science which will be of most use later on, i. e. the economic side.

Even this one aspect of the science covers an enormous amount of ground; and it is profoundly undesirable, even if it were possible, to make an exhaustive study of its innumerable details. On the other hand, the fundamental principles involved are few and comparatively simple; and it is both possible and absolutely essential to grasp these principles firmly and clearly. This knowledge, once made a real possession, can be applied very rapidly and with great certainty to new cases; and, as the strain on the memory is thus minimized, the results seem to be out of all proportion to the initial labour.

The maps in this Atlas are intended to assist such a process. The earlier ones embody the great world-principles which make the necessary *minimum* and foundation, climatic phenomena being specially emphasized because they illustrate best the ordinary processes of Geographic Control. The later maps, being concerned only with commercial products, are the least useful; indeed, they are absolutely useless—and may be even harmful—unless they are used in close connexion with the physical and climatic maps which precede them. So, too, in the case of the economic and industrial maps of the continents; they are intended only as 'comments' on the corresponding plates which give the physical and climatic aspects of the same areas.

GENERAL WORLD-MAPS

All the Economic and Distribution maps of the world are on Gall's Stereographic Cylindrical Projection. This projection has the advantage of representing the relative areas of different parts of the earth's surface with approximate truth, though distortion of shapes is unavoidable towards the poles. Most of the Orographical, Commercial, and Political maps of the world are on Mercator's Projection, its essential defect being—from the purely economic point of view—so far useful in that it helps to give a correct idea, by its exaggeration of the size, of the relatively overwhelming importance of the North Temperate Zone. That is the most important part of the great land hemisphere; the enormous majority of economic products are derived from the land; and the North Temperate Zone was the scene and the source of the earliest stages of economic progress for man. The absence of mountains running north and south in the west of Europe, and the presence of a Monsoon area in the east of Asia, were responsible for the distribution of plant and animal life which led to the relatively speedy development of man in the 'Culture Zone of Eurasia', i. e. an area lying roughly between lines joining Glasgow to Hakodate and the Canary Islands to Formosa (Taiwan).

Pp. 2–3. Bathy-Orographical Chart. The relative areas of land and sea (28 : 72) should, of course, be checked on a globe; but, as a matter of fact, the exaggeration of the land area in the north is practically compensated by the exaggeration of the sea area in the south.

The placing of the Pacific in the centre of the map is not due to the relative importance of the ocean itself, which—except in size—is less important than the Atlantic. But the greatest commercial nations of the world owe their position mainly to the Atlantic; and, to appreciate the reason of the unique importance of the Atlantic, we need to look at a similar map with the Pacific in the centre. Then, if we trace the general course of the great water-parting between the Atlantic and the Indo-Pacific oceans, we find that we have divided the world into two fairly equal parts; and the smaller ocean must obviously have the larger feeding basin. That is to say, almost all the really important rivers in the world empty into the Atlantic.

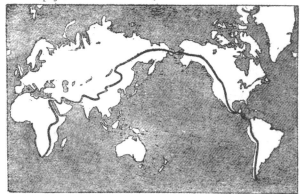

(From Black's *Text-Book of Geography*—by permission.)

The areas coloured green or white are—outside polar regions—specially important. The original home of all important animal forms was near the shore-line, certainly not more than about 600 feet above or below ocean level; and since the distribution of land and water has been that to which we are accustomed, the shallow seas have been the scenes of all the great fishing-grounds, as their shores have been the homes of all the great fishing races; and to-day all the great commercial cities of the world stand on the low land.

P. 4. Isotherms. The isotherms, as here given, are reduced to sea-level temperatures; and, therefore, they need to be corrected by the land heights of the previous map before they give correct ideas of the actual temperature. That is to say, all the land on that map which is not coloured green, has a temperature 2° lower than the corresponding isotherms on this page indicate.

Close comparison of the winter and summer isotherms, especially over the land, will show how misleading a mean temperature may be; indeed, some places never have their allotted 'mean temperature'—except perhaps for a day or two in spring or autumn.

These isotherm maps, like all the other maps, require to be read in close connexion with allied maps before they become really clear or illuminating. For instance, reference to pp. 2–3 shows the limits inside which the actual sun-heat is wasted in melting ice at the sea-level; reference to p. 5 shows how winds may (a) carry oceanic influences inland, e.g. in Western Europe, or (b) carry continental influences seaward, e.g. off Eastern Asia; reference to pp. 6 and 7 shows how the lowering of temperature is due (a) off the west coasts of the southern hemisphere to the upwelling of cold water where the Trade-winds swoop on to the ocean, and (b) off the east coasts of the northern hemisphere to the presence of cold surface currents from polar regions. Generally, it appears that, as the direct influence of the sun decreases, the isotherms coincide less and less with parallels of latitude.

P. 5. Isobars. The most instructive parts of these maps are the Monsoon areas, the essential phenomena of which can be illustrated at any seaside place by the alternation of 'land and sea breezes'. Reference to pp. 2–3 will show how the distribution of pressure is affected, not only by the distribution of land and water, but also by the altitude of the land. Reference to pp. 2–3 and 6–7 also throws light on, e.g., the regularity of the isobars in the Southern Ocean, the presence of a 'high pressure' area over continents in winter, and the presence of a relatively 'high pressure' area over oceans in summer.

The maps show how the rotation of the earth deflects all the regular winds,—the warm light winds that travel away from the equator in upper currents, as well as the cold heavy winds that travel to the equator in lower currents; and it is the centrifugal action set up by this rotation that tends to accumulate air—increasing the pressure by about 1 lb. for every 2,500 feet—over the eastern part of each ocean in the lower temperate latitudes. In this connexion, the position of the British Isles with respect to (a) the permanent 'high pressure' area off the Azores, and (b) the permanent 'low pressure' area off Iceland, is specially worthy of attention.

Pp. 6–7. Natural Vegetation and Ocean Currents. Gall's Projection is used here instead of a Mercator because, although it distorts both shape and direction, it does not materially distort area; and the whole importance of the map lies in its showing (a) the relative influence of the ocean, and (b) the relative areas of the various distributions. In both cases one needs approximation to true size.

Reference to p. 5 shows how intimately the great oceanic currents depend on the regular winds; and reference to p. 9 shows how the sun-warmed surface water is driven westward by the Trades in the Atlantic to a point from which it can be driven on eastward by the Anti-Trades. It is almost true to say that the whole story of the British maritime power is summed up in that one statement. The term 'Gulf Stream' should be confined to the stream of salt water which comes out of the Mexican Gulf through the Florida Strait, and which definitely disappears off the Newfoundland Banks—cut off abruptly during most of the year by the cold Labrador current. Though the current stops, the warm wind-blown drift continues its course eastward until it eventually overflows into the Arctic Ocean—by the same three gaps through which in summer the ice-cold water from the north gravitates southward over the Atlantic.

The 'Natural Vegetation' on this map depends practically on the distribution of rainfall—deserts being areas of no rain, forests being areas of great rain, and grass-lands being areas of little rain; and, therefore, the wind and rainfall maps (pp. 5 and 9) should be studied carefully *before* the vegetation. In this case, as elsewhere in the Atlas, the best order of the maps for printing need not be followed by the student.

The vegetation colouring should be interpreted in the light of (a) the isothermal chart on p. 4, and (b) the various charts of product-distribution towards the end of the Atlas. Quite roughly, it is true to say that the poleward limit of sugar-cane is marked by the 70° line,—that of olives by the 60° line,—that of the vine by the 50° line,—that of wheat by the 40° line,—and that of conifer forests by the 30° line.

This projection, giving practical equality of areas, illustrates also the most important results of the contraction of the earth by secular cooling—contraction from a sphere, i.e. maximum volume with minimum surface, into a tetrahedron, i.e. minimum volume with maximum surface. The shrinking globe gets rid of its surplus surface by sagging on four sides,—thus forming the four ocean basins, and showing a land ring in the northern hemisphere, a water ring in the southern hemisphere, and a tendency for each continent (i.e. the land elevation where the edges of each pair of triangles meet) to be opposite an ocean (i.e. the sag in the centre of each triangle).

P. 8. Commercial Cultivation, i.e. production on a huge scale for purposes of trade and commerce, is the latest stage in the development of Man from nomadism through various stages of natural **Forms of Cultivation.** All the most civilized areas have passed through historic stages corresponding to these natural forms; and the predominant influence underlying the conscious specialization for commercial purposes is climate, with its problems of racial strength, labour supply, facilities for transport, etc. Primitive man, historically and economically, is at the mercy of his environment; and his interests are, therefore, local and narrow and almost entirely related to material needs and processes. Cf. notes on p. 12.

P. 9. Mean Annual Rainfall. This map is the natural sequel to the wind maps on p. 5, when studied in relation to a relief map (pp. 2–3); but, like all 'averages', it may be very misleading. It does show the connexion between wind and rain, the position of deserts, and the total amount of rainfall; but the amount is comparatively of little importance, the really vital matter being the seasonal distribution. For instance, the distribution of natural grass-lands is essentially a result of seasonal rainfall; and the climatic control of cultivation (see p. 8) is equally marked, e. g. areas of summer rain being specially suited to grain, areas of winter rain being specially suited to fruit, and so on. This map, therefore, has little or no economic value until it is carefully compared with the seasonal rainfall maps on pp. 18, 32, 36, 40, 44, and 48. And even then one must remember also that (a) where cold dry air is falling to lower and warmer levels, there must be a deficiency of rain as well as heavier pressure, e. g. along the 'Calms' of Cancer and of Capricorn, and (b) that between these Calms, i. e. roughly in the Tropics, rainfall depends far more on mountains than on cyclonic low-pressure areas. Consequently, we must notice specially (a) the presence of great mountain ranges running north and south in the Tropics, i. e. athwart the Trade-winds, and (b) the distance from the sea at which the westerly winds cease to be rain-bearers in the Temperate Zones.

Ocean Surface Temperatures. Comparison with the maps on p. 4 shows that, in a very general way, land and water are alike in respect of temperature—the temperature of both decreasing with distance from the equator or from sea-level. The important points to notice, therefore, are (a) the distance to which relatively warm water pushes poleward in certain parts of the ocean, and relatively cold water pushes equatorward in other parts, and (b) the way in which enclosed or partially enclosed seas, e. g. the Mediterranean, not only attain a very high surface temperature, but are relatively warm even at great depths, whereas in the open ocean the deep water, even in the Torrid Zone, has a temperature very little above freezing-point.

Pp. 10–11. Commercial Development. This map, especially when compared with the relief maps on pp. 2–3, is a very significant comment on the importance of the Atlantic. The areas most favourable to the early development of man were essentially agricultural areas—(a) that of summer rains in East-Central Asia, where the winters are hard and bracing, and (b) that of winter rains round the Mediterranean, where the winters are mild and enervating. The areas most favourable to modern development are essentially industrial areas in temperate latitudes, with easy access—climatic and commercial—to the ocean, and of a rock formation old enough to contain real coal. And it was the attempts to find a water route connecting the Mediterranean and the Indies that led to (a) the rise of the maritime powers of North-West Europe, (b) the discovery and development of the lands round the Atlantic, and (c) the domination of the world by the White man.

P. 12. Density of Population. This map should be read closely with the preceding one, pp. 10–11. It shows how inexhaustible is the fertility of the alluvial lands in the Monsoon area of South-East Asia, and suggests how adverse that fertility is to development on modern lines. It shows also how workable deposits of coal and iron attract labour, and

suggests how closely modern development depends on easy access to the ocean, e. g. for climatic influences in textile work and for transport in hardware work.

If this map is compared with those of Mean Annual Rainfall and Natural Vegetation, and if the areas of no rain and of constant rain are then eliminated, one has a basis for discussing the relative value of the undeveloped lands of the world, especially if these lands are studied in connexion with the various product maps, pp. 51–64.

Occupations of Mankind. This map also should be compared with those of Mean Annual Rainfall and Natural Vegetation, and with that of Density of Population. Hunters and fishermen naturally like to follow their occupations alone, and their lives, like their prey, must be nomad; but the women, being less nomadic than the men, often supplement the results of the chase with those of primitive agriculture. This occurs most often in tropical lands, where the heat and the moisture will give the maximum result from the minimum effort, e. g. the planting of a banana or manioc shoot, and where crops ripen all the year round.

Ordinary agriculture, which begins with the raising of crops from seed, and modern stock-raising, which depends intimately on railway transport, are definitely scientific occupations; and their success makes possible the existence of mining and manufacturing industries. The connexion between the agriculture and the stock-raising is now very close, as stock are fattened on definitely agricultural products, e. g. oil-cake; and neither of them shows its old influence on the dress, dwellings, &c., of the people engaged in it. Railways make it impossible for the modern ranchers to feel the independence, the isolation, the fatalism of the old Steppe nomads.

P. 13. Races of Mankind. This map should be compared with the climatic maps and with that of the Commercial Development of the World—by the White man from the eastern shores of the North Atlantic.

The three varieties of man are specialized forms of a common type, the specific variations being due apparently to the climatic character of the zoological areas over which they respectively spread. The migrations from the common home, somewhere in south-western Asia, were probably begun before the great Ice Age, and were not concluded till that Age had completely passed away. In the intervening ages since then the several varieties have formed distinct racial characters by slow adaptation to their special geographic environment; and, quite roughly, we may say that in the Negro we see the geographic control of damp heat, in the Yellow man (whether Mongol or Amerind) we see the geographic control of an essentially continental climate, and in the White man we see the geographic control of a temperate peninsula.

The economic importance of race, as of religion, is very great. For instance, in the case of the Negro, climatic influences—acting direct and through the typical food—lead to the early closing of the 'seams' between the bones of the skull; and thus the development of the brain is arrested, and the adult is essentially unintellectual. On the other hand, he is naturally 'acclimatized' against numerous diseases and other conditions of life and work which are very adverse to the White man. He is, therefore, of great use as a manual labourer in a 'steamy' climate, e. g. on a cane-sugar plantation.

Religions of Mankind. There are, of course, direct economic results of religious customs, e. g. a demand for fish in Roman Catholic countries, a demand for coffee (in place of alcohol) in Mohammedan countries, a demand for vegetable (in place of animal) food in Hindustan, &c. But, apart from these broad considerations, religious influences may be most intricate and far-leading. For instance, in Turkey there is difficulty in getting a passport on a Friday, for it has to be got from a Moslem,—difficulty in getting your boots cleaned on a Saturday, as most of the boot-blacks are Hebrew,—difficulty in getting a Christian to do work for you on Sunday, and so on. Where race and language are much mixed, creed often has a very great political influence.

SPECIAL MAPS

Pp. 18–19. Europe. In this set of maps, as in the corresponding sets for the other continents, the particular arrangement of the plates is due only to mechanical considerations. In the case of each set, the best procedure would be—first, to compare the Orography plate with the corresponding parts of the maps on pp. 2–5; then, to study the four Climatic plates, with special reference to the Vegetation plate; and lastly, to estimate the relative value of the various units in the Political map by reference to the Vegetation and Population plates.

Comparison of the Orography and the Political plates suggests the importance of fishing as the fundamental basis of maritime power, whether shown in commercial development or colonial empire.

Pp. 20–21. In these detailed Economic and Industrial maps, as in the corresponding maps of the other continents, the relative importance of products can scarcely be judged except by reference to the Population map. For instance, typical exports of grain come only from countries where the population (a) is not dense, and (b) does not consume the particular grain as its standard bread-stuff; thus, wheat is a typical export from the Ukraine, with its normally rye-eating population. Again, fine textile work, especially in cotton and flax, always has a climatic basis, a damp climate being absolutely essential to the spinning of really fine yarn; so that, e. g., cotton and linen manufactures far inland must be mainly of coarse or open-work fabrics, and probably depend on imports of foreign yarn. (Cf. pp. 26–27.)

The colouring on p. 20, as on similar maps throughout the atlas, must not be considered final or exclusive. For instance, barley is grown even inside the Arctic Circle, and wheat is by no means confined to the areas enclosed in blue lines (cf. p. 51). But the colouring does indicate the most important areas in question.

Pp. 22–25. British Isles. The climatic control of textile, as of agricultural, work can be well studied in these maps of the British Isles, by comparing the Mean Annual Rainfall map with the maps of agriculture and textiles. Comparison of the maps on pp. 22 and 24 illustrates the relation of altitude to fertility, ease of transport, and other conditions favourable to the growth of population; and comparison of the two temperature maps illustrates the typical differences between marine and continental conditions.

Pp. 26–27. The great railway routes show that the relation of the great plain to the Alpine system has not deprived it of its essential advantage as a typical piece of Atlantic hinterland; for the distribution of the highlands puts little obstacle to access—commercial or climatic—to and from the Atlantic, while their character minimizes the obstacle to commerce between the complementary 'summer-rain' and 'summer-drought' sections of the continent without depriving the latter of its shelter from cold northern blasts. The ends of the crystalline ranges of the Alps were thin enough to be easily tunnelled, e. g. at the Simplon and St. Gothard foci; and, as the mass of the mineral wealth of the continent is found in or near the northern scarp of the old crustal blocks of Central Europe, the line of minimum resistance to human movement—just north of the old blocks—has been also the line of maximum convenience for the working of the minerals. Rhine and Rhone, Danube and Ticino, draw their summer floods from the neighbourhood of the St. Gothard; and it is possible to travel from Bayonne to Warsaw *via* Paris and Berlin, *round* the old blocks without going through a single tunnel and without ever being 600 feet above sea-level. This fact makes it absurd to compare continental with British canals or to draw 'lessons' from the former for the latter. Between Berlin and Hamburg (230 miles) there are only three locks; the average in England is one lock for every 1200 yards of canal!

Pp. 28–29. The Mediterranean basin forms a natural area between the Alps and the Sahara, and has, therefore, a natural 'monopoly' of certain ('summer-drought') products, which gives it special economic importance; and the sea itself has the commercial advantage of being four times as long as it is wide. Its coast is more broken, and has better outlets, on the European than on the non-European side; and the through route is essentially a 'coastal' one, not admitting of great-circle sailing nor being really oceanic. It is fed from a number of bays, and the length of these has led to the development of a number of separate foci at the maximum distance from the through route, e. g. Marseilles and Genoa, Venice and Constantinople, more or less subordinate to a few others actually on the direct route, e. g. Gibraltar and Algiers, Malta and Suez. And the number of heavy cargoes 'out' from the European ports guarantees that imported coal will be cheap everywhere—an immense advantage to shipping, but one that tends to accentuate the tendency for commerce to concentrate on a few very large centres.

Pp. 30–35. Asia. The total distance from Petrograd to Vladivostok by the Trans-Siberian Railway is about 5,500 miles—fully 30 of which are over bridges; and the distance to Peking by the same line is about 6,000 miles, i. e. *less* than that from London to Bombay via Suez.

The ultimate importance of the Trans-Siberian Railway, however, is probably much less than that of the various

'Baghdad' routes. The obvious route is via the Euphrates. But the old military roads, like modern economic railways, made Mosul their objective, thus increasing the importance of Aleppo (and Antioch) at the expense of Damascus.

Aleppo is now the pivot of the whole Asiatic hinterland of the Levant; and, though it has as yet no railway connexions along two of its old caravan routes—to Trebizond and down the Euphrates valley, it has such connexions for its three other great routes—to Scutari, Medina, and Mosul. The Anatolian route appealed to the Germans on strategic grounds, but the proper route for trade is the one chosen by Lord Beaconsfield in 1879—from Alexandretta direct via Nisibin for Mosul across the *southern*[1] end of the Giaur Dagh.

There is a contract for the carrying of the Indian mails from England, which is most important in relation to the prosperity of our Mercantile Marine; and the transference of the mails to a 'Mesopotamian' railway would be a mistake, even if the line were our own. In any case the railway could not deliver the mails any quicker than the P. & O. boats can, and it would carry them through areas both in Europe and in Asia which cannot compare with West Europe in, e. g. security for life and property; and the cost by land would be enormously greater.

Reference to the population map on p. 33 shows that there was practically no chance of the 'German' line being financially successful. Even in Anatolia it runs through an area where the average population does not exceed 15 per square mile; and for over two-thirds of the rest of the route to Baghdad it would run through areas where the average does not exceed 5 per square mile.

P. 34. Such products as tea and coffee are appropriate to a Monsoon area, not only for direct climatic reasons, but also because the cheapness of food, with the consequent dense population, means cheap labour.

Rice and millet are respectively 'wet' and 'dry' crops, while rice and wheat are respectively 'summer' and 'winter' crops; and opium has a close connexion with rice-growing, the preliminary stages of the rice cultivation causing rheumatic troubles which can be alleviated by opium.

Comparison of the political map (p. 33) with the maps on p. 13 suggests one of the most interesting of political problems—the future of Asia. In the north—speaking very broadly—the White man is ruling the Yellow man with a purely continental empire; in the south, the White man is ruling the White man, with a purely marine empire; in the west, the Yellow man, from a buffer position between the continental and the marine empires, is ruling the White man. Will the Yellow man in the east, in virtue of his marine power, rule the Yellow man?

Pp. 36–39. Africa. The character and distribution of the typical products, e. g. rubber and ivory, palm-oil and dates, should be studied in close relation with the climatic maps. Where the exportable wealth is of 'jungle' character, e. g. rubber, palm-oil, and ivory, the waterways became—and still are—of prime importance, because on the land routes—previous to the invention of some means of transport not affected by the tsetse-fly—human labour was the only 'animal'

[1] The Germans chose the northern end because the Issus plain is exposed to 'sea power'.

labour possible. Where the climate is influenced by a cold current and off-shore winds, we have such typical products as guano and fish (cf. the name *Walvis* = 'Whale-fish') in the same latitudes as the Chilian nitrate-grounds and fisheries. A typically intermediate climate, with corresponding products, is found along the route of the 'Cape-to-Cairo' railway, the completed part of which follows a line of volcanic disturbance along the Indo-Atlantic water-parting; and this disturbance has resulted in the wide distribution of mineral wealth, as in the crater-chimneys of the Kimberley diamond mines.

Pp. 40–43. North America. Comparison of the industrial map with the climatic maps suggests—what is actually the fact—that the northern limit of agriculture in N.W. Canada is fixed, not by climatic considerations, but by economic, e. g. transport, labour, &c. The lie of this Central Canadian agricultural land represents the natural trend of the real 'prairie', the semi-arid region between the real prairies and the Rockies narrowing northwards, thus giving Canada an advantage over the United States. The climatic line between the cotton belt and the maize is decided not by summer heat, but by winter cold (see p. 40). It is typical of the conditions that Cairo is the first really *unhealthy* town as you descend the Mississippi; but the map does not distinguish between the 'fine' and 'coarse cotton' areas. Cf. note on p. 60.[1]

Pp. 44–46. South America. The economic importance of the continent is largely due to the peculiarity of its relief—as affecting transport and vegetation. Two-thirds of the area is in the Tropics, half of it being less than 600 feet above the sea, while a large proportion of the rest is more than 10,000 feet. Reference to the maps of Natural Vegetation and Seasonal Rainfall (pp. 45 and 47) will show the relation of summer rains not only to the actual existence of the grass-lands, but also to the development of grain-growing on them, especially the growing of wheat on the pampa.

Pp. 47–53. The map on p. 47 should not be studied till the first six maps on the two following pages have been carefully studied. In both Australia and New Zealand wool is much the most valuable export, wheat coming second in Australia, and frozen meat or butter second in New Zealand. Butter is important in both countries, though the climate of Australia is (cf. p. 48) typically continental, while that of New Zealand is typically oceanic; in the latter dairy products as a whole come even before wool.

Pp. 51–60. These charts of plant distribution should be studied mainly as instances of climatic control. Soil is of comparatively little importance, as the usual deficiencies of soils can be made good by scientific tillage and treatment—so as to suit more or less all ordinary crops.

P. 51. For instance, spring *wheat* is essentially a 'continental' crop, the product of early summer rains, as in America and Russia. As these rains are due to the formation

[1] Here, as elsewhere, the various items on the continental maps should be studied closely in connexion with the charts of their general distribution (pp. 51–64), and the notes on the same (p. x). In view of the abnormal economic conditions in recent years it is obviously impossible at present to give in these charts perfectly satisfactory averages, but an attempt has been made to present careful approximations to the actual facts.

of 'low pressure' areas as the sun-heat increases, the mass of the rain (¾ of the total fall on the prairies) falls precisely when the young wheat needs it most ; and, as the decrease of temperature in autumn naturally stops the inflow of the warm wet winds, harvest time is normally dry. The French crop—of winter wheat—is important because its quantity depends on the semi-marine character of the winter in France, while its quality depends on the largely continental character of the summer. The Indian crop is winter wheat in a different sense—it *ripens* in 'winter', the cool and dry season ; and its distribution depends entirely on the length of the cool season—the Indian wheats being very speedy ripeners. The importance of the Indian crop lies largely in the fact that a large part of it is intended for export, the local population consuming rice in the typically damp areas and millet in the typically dry areas. Cheapness of land and of transport are important points in connexion with the American crop, while cheapness of labour is important in connexion with the Russian and Indian crops.

P. 52. *Maize* is also closely connected with summer-rain areas in warm temperate latitudes, e. g. along the Dniester, Danube, Plate, and Mississippi ; but it has a much smaller climatic range than wheat, and—as its special use is as food for cattle and 'hogs'—its export depends largely on very cheap transport.

Barley has a wider climatic range (both in latitude and in altitude) than any other cereal, and is probably the most ancient of cultivated grasses. It does well wherever wheat flourishes, e. g. in Russia ; but the best qualities come from areas of summer drought, i. e. 'Mediterranean' climates, especially from Asia Minor and California.

Oats prefer a cool and moist climate, *rice* prefers a hot and moist one ; oats, therefore, are specially suitable for areas of light rain evenly distributed throughout the year, e. g. Ireland and Scotland, while rice is most suitable for Monsoon areas, especially low-lying areas that can be easily flooded, e. g. the deltas and flood-plains of great rivers. But oats enter much the more largely into commerce, because rice is essentially consumed where it is grown, its presence accounting for the dense population of the typical Monsoon areas. The importance of the rice-crop of Burma is due precisely to the relatively small population, which leaves a large surplus for export. Cf. p. 34.

Commercially, *maize* bears somewhat the same relation to *barley* as rice does to oats, but its local consumption gives a clue to the number of animals, especially cattle and pigs, not to the human population.

P. 53. *Potatoes* and *Sago* offer a good contrast. The potato illustrates well the importance of using the term 'Natural Product' with a special meaning in Economic Geography. As the amount of available unoccupied land decreases, the need increases for using occupied land in the best possible way. This is probably done most satisfactorily by using it, e. g., for such plants as are 'Natural Products' —in the sense of indigenous to the particular place ; for instance, the best rubber will probably be obtained from plants artificially cultivated in areas where rubber grows, or has grown, wild. The term 'Natural Product', therefore,

may be taken to describe a product raised perhaps artificially, but under essentially natural and appropriate conditions, as distinguished from an 'Unnatural Product', i. e. one raised under unnatural and inappropriate conditions.

The potato is a native of the high and dry Andean plateau, but has extraordinary powers of acclimatization provided the sun-heat is not materially greater than in its native home ; so that it can be grown at sea-level in high latitudes, in either moist or dry climates.

The sago palm is a native of the East Indies, and the whole supply for the world practically comes from the eastern half of the archipelago—in sacks made out of the leaves of the palm. As a plantation renews itself, and even extends itself, without human labour, and as it ripens at all seasons of the year, and gives an enormous amount of food-pith, it puts a premium on laziness. The oil-palm, especially in West Africa, is equally valuable on the spot, and even more so as providing an export (palm-oil) to Europe.

Dates and *coconuts*[1] are lovers respectively of dry heat and damp heat—the one being essentially at home in tropical deserts, the other on tropical shores ; the one is, therefore, a typically continental plant, while the other is typically oceanic. Both are exceedingly useful where they grow, the coconut providing juice for 'milk', nut-shells for cups and bowls, fibre for 'coir' rope and mats, leaves for thatching, wood for oars, boats, houses, &c. The coir and copra (dried kernels) enter much more largely into commerce than do the products of the date-palm ; and, of course, islands are infinitely more accessible than deserts.

P. 54. Not only is the essential property to which *tea*, *coffee*, and *cacao* owe their stimulating value practically the same in each case, but in other respects also they have much in common. All three require a rich, light, friable soil, with abundance of 'humus' in or on top of it ; they all need frequent heavy rains, but a well-drained subsoil ; they all derive great benefit from shade. A favourable site would, therefore, be a clearing in a forest on the side of a hill exposed to Trade-wind or Monsoon rains. Again, they all demand a great deal of labour, which must be both cheap and not clumsy ; for instance, in picking cacao it is most important to avoid injuring the buds and blossoms which are to give the next harvest. They are alike again in not giving an immediate return on cultivation, the planter having to wait from three years (for tea) to twelve (for some kinds of cacao—or cocoa) before seeing any real profit. These conditions combine to limit the distribution of the products very materially, e. g. climate often being suitable where there is no cheap good labour.

On the contrary, there are interesting differences between the plants, especially from the climatic point of view. For instance, the *tea* is a shrub, and its value is in the leaf ; and, as the leaves are best when they are young, the best are usually[2] picked in 'Spring'. The plant is also essentially

[1] This is the only correct spelling, as the tree has nothing to do with the *cocoa* or *cacao* tree. The word *coco* is allied to *cockle*, and refers to the shape of the nut-shells.

[2] In Ceylon, where 'winter is only a word', picking goes on the whole year through ; in India it is confined more or less to the time of the S. W. Monsoon.

a sub-tropical plant—one of the hardiest of all such plants; and, therefore, it has a wide climatic range, even being able to stand severe frost. This accounts for its flourishing in the temperate area of S. E. Asia. There are two kinds of tea-plants, highland and lowland, the former being the finer, but the latter the more productive; and there are two kinds of tea, black and green, the difference being entirely due to the process of manufacture. Thus, green tea may be made from the so-called 'Black Tea-plant' (Thea Bohea) of the Canton district, and black tea may be made from the so-called 'Green Tea-plant' (Thea *viridis*) of the Chekiang district.

The *coffee* is also a shrub, but considerably larger than the tea; it is also of two kinds, highland and lowland, the 'Arabian' highland kind being much the finer, especially in aroma, but the 'Liberian' lowland kind being the more prolific. The plant has not as wide a climatic range as the tea, being very sensitive to cold and to hot dry winds. On the other hand, its value is in the fruit, not the leaf; and the most perfectly ripened fruit comes from dry and hot areas, where the berries can be allowed to mature until they drop off. This accounts for the excellence of Bolivian and real Mocha coffee, as the constant warmth and moisture account for the excellence of the 'Blue Mountains' crop in Jamaica. Like the tea, the plant must be protected from heavy winds; and it also requires shade from the sun, this being provided for the Mocha plants by the mid-day mists off the steaming waters that wash the Yemen coast. Access to the sea is always important, however, as coffee is grown essentially for export, not for local use.

The *cacao*, or cocoa tree, is more tropical even than the coffee, having the typical 'wet-jungle' habit of bearing its fruit on its *stem*, i. e. the part of the tree most accessible—in dense jungle—to the insects which fertilize the flowers. It is also more sensitive to exposure than the coffee, being peculiarly sensitive to winds of all kinds, especially winds off salt water; it also, unlike tea and coffee, prefers a volcanic soil. The cacao, therefore, grows normally as much nearer to the equator than the coffee as the coffee does normally than the tea; and there is no 'highland' variety. The deep, moist, volcanic valleys of Central America and the Northern Andes are the ideal site for cacao.

Sugar-cane is like cacao in its preference for lowlands and for volcanic soil, but it has a wider climatic range than even coffee; it is never found along with tea, as it must have easy access to lime, which is absent from typical 'tea' soils. The most suitable climate is one where hot moist weather alternates with periods of hot dry weather, especially where there is salt in the air or in the soil. It is, therefore, very much at home in mountainous islands inside the tropics; and on the windward shores of such islands it is almost the only profitable crop. In India it is grown mainly for local use, the great exporting areas being essentially islands, e. g. Java and Cuba, Hawaii and Mauritius.

Sugar-beet resembles sugar-cane in its apparent liking for a saltish soil, but it could scarcely compete with the cane except for the extraordinary amount of 'artificial' encouragement which it has received from the governments of Central Europe. It certainly can be grown close to dense manu-

facturing populations in temperate latitudes, where capital, markets, machinery, and manure are accessible; but it is only an annual, it requires careful cultivation—in areas where labour is relatively dear, and it is not nearly so rich as the cane in sugar.

P. 55. The *banana* is one of the most nutritious, as well as probably the most prolific, of all food plants. The banana and the plantain are respectively what may be called the 'fruit' and the 'vegetable' varieties of the same plant; both are of various sizes, are perennials, and yield a return within a year.

While the banana is typically the product of a marine climate—being often used as a shade tree for cacao plantations—the *apple* is typically a 'continental' product, flourishing best where the spring is so short that the plant cannot make both wood and fruit successfully, and where the sudden and short autumn stops the rising of sap directly the crop has been gathered. These continental climates have also, as a rule, dry weather in the late summer and early autumn—when the 'low pressure' is failing (cf. p. vii); and this is very favourable to the quality and the keeping of the apple, as it is also to the development of sugar in the sugar-beet—a reason for *not* growing sugar-beet in England.

The *orange* is probably a native of China, where it is still very largely cultivated and consumed; but it is most prolific in tropical and semi-tropical climates. As, at the same time, it is very widely consumed in temperate climates, it has a distinct commercial importance. As a native of a summer-rain climate, its acclimatization in a climate of summer-drought—the Mediterranean area, from which the mass of the British supply comes—has been easy because of its love of bright sunshine and 'generous' soil; but the flavour of most of these 'Mediterranean' oranges is much inferior to that of the 'West Indian', especially the Jamaican, fruit. A single tree in Jamaica may bear 10,000 oranges; and, as the crop begins to ripen as early as September, the fruit can reach the British market before even that from the irrigated parts of the Mediterranean, and is much sweeter than any artificially hastened fruit can ever be.

The *spice* trade is more interesting for historic than commercial reasons. The demand for spices was relatively greater in days when the preservation of fish and meat for winter food depended entirely on the use of spice; and in those days there were enormous profits in the trade because of the extraordinary difference in the value of the product in its place of origin—a tropical island—and in the European market, Vasco da Gama's spice-cargo from India in 1497 yielding a profit of 6,000 per cent.

Nearly all spices are natives of S. E. Asia, nutmegs and cloves being specifically Molucca ('Spice Islands') products, while pepper is specifically Indian, and cinnamon Cingalese. Nowadays the mass of the pepper imported into the United Kingdom comes from the Malabar coast or via Singapore from the Straits Settlements and the Dutch East Indies. Nearly all the ginger comes from Jamaica, but cardamoms (the fruit, as opposed to the root, of a 'ginger') come still from the East Indies. Nutmegs, again, still come from the East Indies; but cloves, which are very sensitive to sea-winds, come specially from Zanzibar. Almost all real cinnamon, which—like ginger—demands a very rich soil, comes from Ceylon; pimento, which likes a very poor soil, comes from the 'barren land' of Jamaica.

P. 56. *Sheep* and goats, for wool-making purposes, require a dry temperate climate tending to warmth, where the 'fat' is not needed, and consumed, to keep up the bodily heat. This accounts for the importance of 'Mediterranean' climates. The merino was a native of North Africa, greatly improved in Spain, and (after having been acclimatized in Saxony with still further improvement) eventually transferred with complete success to other 'Mediterranean' latitudes—in Australia, South Africa, the Argentine, &c. The best merino wool is now very long in staple, quite unlike that of the original merino. Mutton, as opposed to wool, is the product rather of a damp climate, such as is typical of temperate islands; and, as the merino yields a very poor 'continental' type of mutton, the attempt was made to breed a 'cross' between the mutton-producing and the wool-producing types. All areas which export both wool and mutton, e.g. New Zealand, are bound to patronize largely this cross-breed. Wool from countries which produce neither good mutton nor good wool is mainly used for blankets (Indian) and carpets (Chinese). The product of the camels'-hair district in Russia is used for belting (for machinery).

P. 57. There is practically the same difference in quality between 'insular' and 'continental' beef as between 'insular' and 'continental' mutton; but, while the sheep is essentially a hill animal, *cattle* are essentially lowlanders. The value of land restricts the spread of pasture in densely-peopled countries, where the demand for milk and meat is greatest; and artificial means of preserving food have not yet completely revolutionized the natural distributions. Cattle are raised in the United States, Germany, and the Plate district, mainly for meat; in India and South Africa for draught-work; in Russia and Brazil for hides, bones, and tallow; in Western Europe and Eastern Canada specially for dairy purposes. Apart from cattle, horses, sheep, goats, and pigs are the chief source of hides and skins; and the special interest of the *Hides and Skins* chart lies in tracing the connexion between the quantity exported and (*a*) the extent of cheap pasture-land, (*b*) the low price of labour, (*c*) the standard of agricultural science, (*d*) the distribution of tanning materials—Australasian hides and skins, for instance, generally coming to England untanned.

The great cattle-belt in U.S.A. extends along the eastern foot of the Rocky Mountains from Iowa to Texas; in Germany, Bavaria and Saxony are the great areas; in India there is a typical area of light rainfall and saltish soil from Cutch to Kashmir, the seaward half of which makes Rajputana the great cattle-ground.

P. 58. Reference to the earlier physical maps will draw attention to the importance in fishing industries of shallow sea, especially of large submarine banks (1) near enough to the surface of the sea to be covered with the seaweed in which the fish can find their food, lay their eggs, &c., and (2) near enough to deep water for the fish to be able to take refuge from storms and cold weather. The connexion should also be noticed of (1) cold currents with improved quality of product, and (2) warm surface currents with distribution of the eggs, the current in the North Sea distributing them first to Scotland and England, then to Holland and Germany, and last of all to Scandinavia.

P. 59. The *vine* is another of those products the distribution of which depends almost as much on economic as on climatic control. Its climatic range is practically dependent on the length of the summer and the natural sun-heat in the late summer and early autumn, successful cultivation (for wine-making) in Europe requiring an average maximum temperature of 60° F. in September. On the other hand, the severity of the winter is of little or no importance, the length of the root taking it beyond the reach of almost the severest frost, as it also takes it beyond the reach of almost the severest drought. The sun-heat must not be too great, or the wine becomes syrupy; nor too little, or it becomes vinegary. The most appropriate site is, therefore, a slope of from 30° to 45°, facing rather eastward as well as sunward, in latitudes 40–50° N. and 30–40° S.

Inside these limits wine-making is mainly confined to warm soils which are retentive of moisture, e.g. chalk, in lands where there is abundance of (*a*) capital, (*b*) skilled labour, (*c*) cheap chemical manures, insecticides, &c. France is far the most important country in amount produced, amount consumed locally (at least 25 gallons *per caput per annum*), and amount exported; but Italy has much the largest area under vines (half as much land as all the grain crops combined), and the total estimated value of the crop is greater than that of the French. The diagram needs, therefore, to be interpreted in the light of two further facts— (1) that the amount of alcohol in 'Mediterranean', i.e. 'summer-drought', wines is at least 50 per cent. higher even than that in French wines, and (2) that only some 2 per cent. of the total production of French wine can be graded higher than *vin ordinaire*.

A careful study of the climatic conditions round Cognac and Cadiz will suggest reasons for sherry being the richest of all wines in organic ethers, and for French brandy having a higher percentage of such ethers than any other so-called brandy.

Tobacco, as a native of tropical America, obviously must like heat and humidity; but it is a hardy plant—though sensitive to frost—and most of the tobacco of commerce is raised in distinctly temperate latitudes. In all cases, however, it thrives best on light soil that is rich in lime and humus, especially if potash is also present in abundance. The ideal site, therefore, would be a coral-girt volcanic island in the tropics; and the best-flavoured leaves of temperate regions come from areas of (once forested) limestone within 40° of the equator.

The best cigars must be made from the fresh leaf—one reason for purely 'marine' tobaccos, e.g. from Cuba, Sumatra, Manila, being used specially for cigars. On the contrary, most imported leaves will be used for pipe tobacco, manufactured where they are imported; and, for this purpose, purely 'continental' tobaccos are specially suitable, e.g. products of the Ohio, the upper Danube, the upper Garonne districts.

'Semi-marine' tobaccos, especially from areas of summer drought and winter-rain, e. g. the Syrian and Anatolian and Turkish coastlands, the delta of Egypt, and Virginia (U.S.A.), where leaf of very light shade is produced, are most suitable for cigarettes. In each case, however, the quality of the leaf varies with the soil—excess of lime, for instance, giving quantity at the expense of quality, while excess of clay, e. g. in Chinese loess, gives a very light yellow leaf that has practically no taste at all. The percentage of nicotine seems to be a climatic result, varying from 2 per cent. in a good 'marine' leaf, e. g. from the Vuelta-abajo of Cuba, to 9 or 10 per cent. in a common 'continental' leaf, e. g. from S.W. Germany.

P. 60. *Cotton*, like tobacco, has a considerable climatic range, though it too is sensitive to frost; and it grows best on light limestone soils in warm, moist, even climates, where the summer is long, and where there is salt in the soil or in the air. It is the most important of all 'sub-tropical' plants, and has a wide climatic range, much more than half the total crop in the world being grown in temperate latitudes. The largest amounts are grown in China and the United States, i. e. essentially 'continental' areas; but the finest quality comes from 'marine' climates, e. g. the sea-islands along the U.S.A. coast between Charleston and Savannah, the Nile delta, and various islands just inside the tropics, where the heat is not excessive, e. g. the Fijis. The U.S.A. 'sea-island' cotton is gathered from the *Gossypium Barbadense* plant, and Barbados and other West Indian islands a century ago provided far more than half the total crop of the world. Brazil cotton resembles West Indian in length, but the greater heat makes it rather coarser; the short-staple Indian cotton suffers also from excessive heat and from want of bright sunshine during the Monsoon summer; the fine and long Egyptian product profits by abundance of bright sunshine, while the water-supply is regulated by irrigation.

As to the increase of supply in the future, the Eastern and Central Sudan can grow unlimited quantities of cotton of the Egyptian type, the West Indies can do the same with regard to sea-island fibre, and Brazil, Northern Nigeria, Nyasaland, and Uganda can do the same with cotton of the American 'upland' type. But a high relative humidity is more useful than the finest irrigation works; total amount of rainfall is of no importance compared with its seasonal distribution, rain in spring being essential to the development of stem and leaf, while rain in late summer—such as is typical of many parts of West Africa—diverts energy from the production of bolls if it does not actually rot the pods; and islands have obvious advantages of transport and freedom from frost.

Rubber till 1911 was almost entirely 'wild'; the world's output was under 75,000 tons, and *c.* 45 per cent. of this came from Brazil. By 1920 the total output was 325,000 tons, only the 'odd' 25,000 was—'wild'—from Brazil, and practically all the rest was plantation rubber, more than half coming from Malaya and about a quarter from Sumatra and Java. With Ceylon, the British Empire now supplies, therefore, nearly 65 per cent. of the world's demand.

Flax grows best on the leaf-mould of deciduous forests;

but its use varies with the mean temperature, the fibre being very poor where the seed produces good oil. In Russia it has the largest area of any crop, partly because it was grown originally to satisfy the demand for a vegetable oil—in place of butter—during the fasts of the Greek Church. The fibre was, therefore, in the nature of a by-product; and Russia thus came to supply nearly four-fifths of the world's demand for the fibre. But Calcutta is—or has been till recently—the great linseed-oil market. The finest fibre is grown on the alluvial soil of Flanders, where too the quality of the water, especially in the Lys, is very favourable to the retting of the fibre; but that grown on the Po delta, especially round Cremona, is also very good. The plant requires a great deal of cheap labour both on the field and—for fibre—in its earlier manufacturing processes; and this accounts both for its wide cultivation in Northern Italy, Russia, and other countries where labour is cheap, and where women do hard out-of-door labour, and for the fact that, where labour is dear, the plant is grown for oil even though the climate is really unsuitable, e.g. U.S.A. As the inset diagram shows only the production of the fibre, it does not indicate the commercial importance of the enormous areas under the plant in the Argentine and the United States.

Hemp is grown under very similar conditions, but has to be produced even more cheaply. Russia, again, supplies most of the fibre, while the best comes from the Bologna district of Italy; and, again, 'Monsoon' Asia supplies the other products of the plant, mainly various stimulants. The henequen, or so-called 'hemp' exported from Yucatan via Sisal, is an agave product; and the Manila 'hemp' of the Philippines comes from a kind of plantain.

Pp. 61–64. These mineral charts, though useful in giving a bird's-eye view of the general distribution of the minerals, are of little educational value unless they can be studied in reference to geological maps of the various areas.

Coal is always found along with sediments which have been laid down under water, but close to dry land; and generally a seam is overlaid by water-bearing sandstone, and underlaid by impervious slate or clay. The outcrop is, therefore, often marked by a line of marshy ground; and the presence of fossils of 'Carboniferous Age' is a reasonable guarantee of the presence of coal underground.

Petroleum—and the same is true of natural gas—is generated by accumulations of organic remains, similar to those which are the source of coal; these accumulations are found in porous rock, e. g. coarse sandstone, but the impervious layer (of clay) is above, not below, so that the resultant fluid has not escaped to the surface.

In the case of *metals*, the beds of ore, e. g. of gold and magnetic iron, are largely the result of volcanic action, occurring as the result of the precipitation of metal from warm water, while the true veins, e. g. of copper, silver, lead, are largely the result of plutonic action, having been filled by sublimation, i. e. the temporary vaporizing of the metal in its original site, or some similar process. The common metals are found in rocks of every geological age, but are seldom found pure.

UNIVERSITY COLLEGE, LONDON.   L. W. L.
October, 1924.

LIST OF MAPS

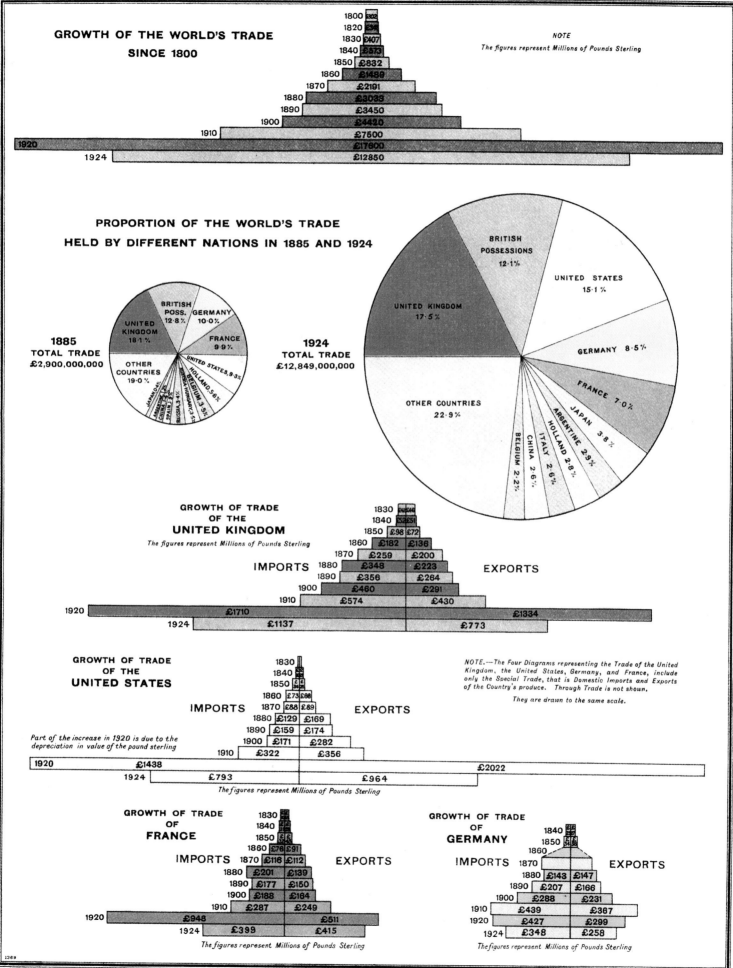

GROWTH OF THE WORLD'S TRADE
SINCE 1800

The Edinburgh Geographical Institute

John Bartholomew & Son Ltd

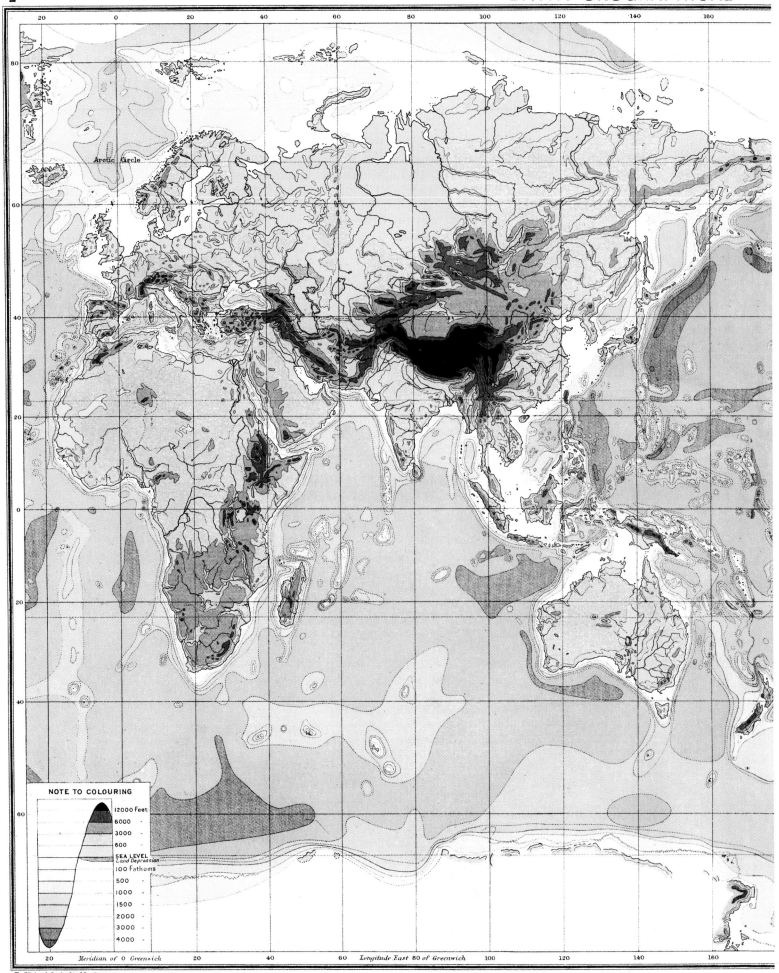

NOTE TO COLOURING

12000 Feet
6000
3000
600
SEA LEVEL
Land Depression
100 Fathoms
500
1000
1500
2000
3000
4000

Arctic Circle

Meridian of O Greenwich   Longitude East 80 of Greenwich

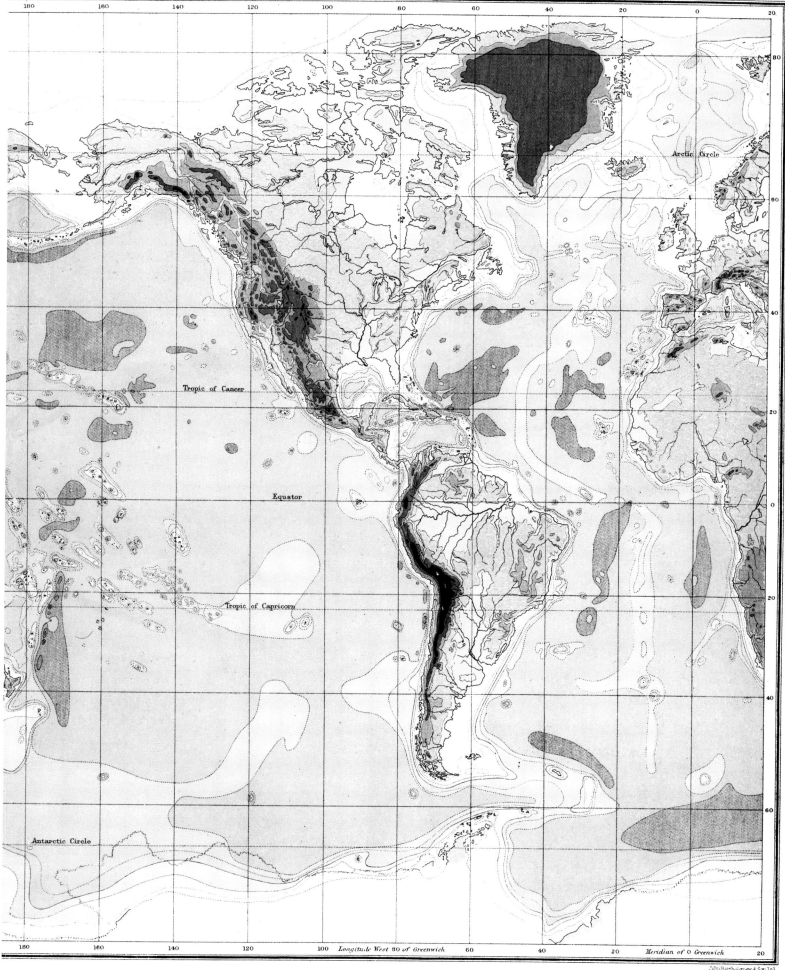

Arctic Circle

Tropic of Cancer

Equator

Tropic of Capricorn

Antarctic Circle

Meridian of 0 Greenwich

John Bartholomew & Son,Ltd.

Projection

CLIMATE

Arctic Circle
Tropic of Cancer
Equator
Tropic of Capricorn
Antarctic Circle

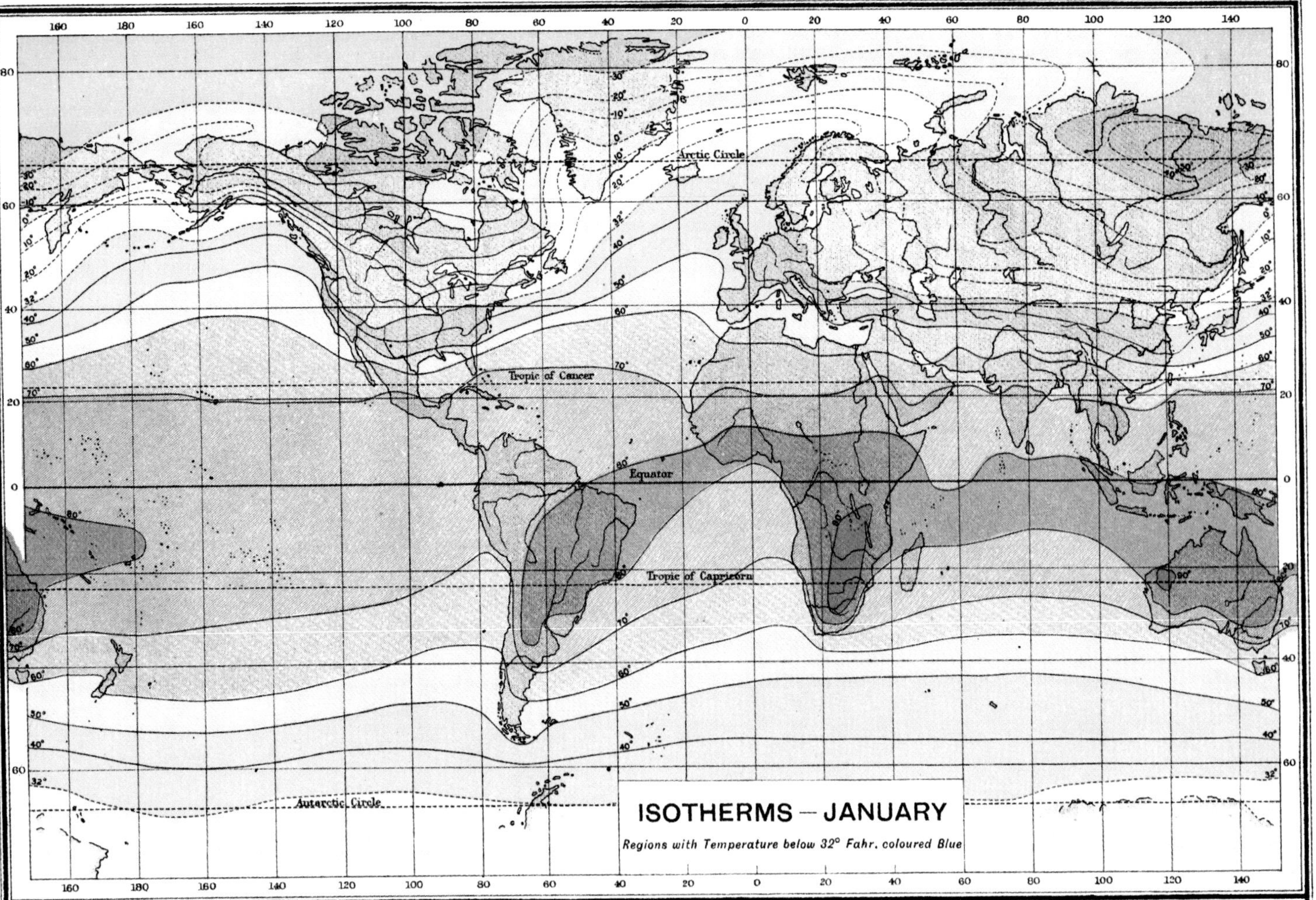

ISOTHERMS – JANUARY

Regions with Temperature below 32° Fahr. coloured Blue

Arctic Circle
Tropic of Cancer
Equator
Tropic of Capricorn
Antarctic Circle

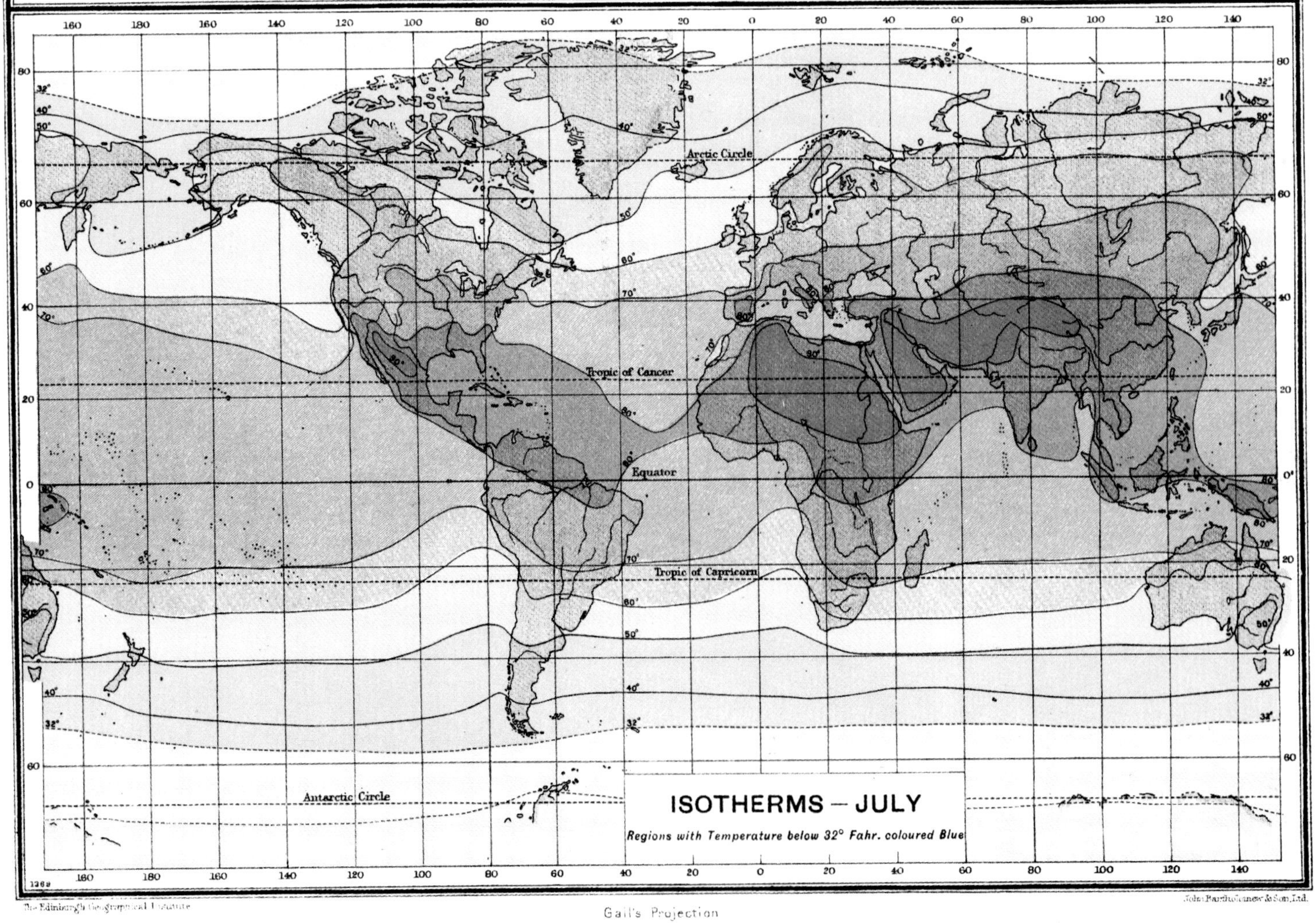

ISOTHERMS – JULY

Regions with Temperature below 32° Fahr. coloured Blue

The Edinburgh Geographical Institute

John Bartholomew & Son, Ltd.

Gall's Projection

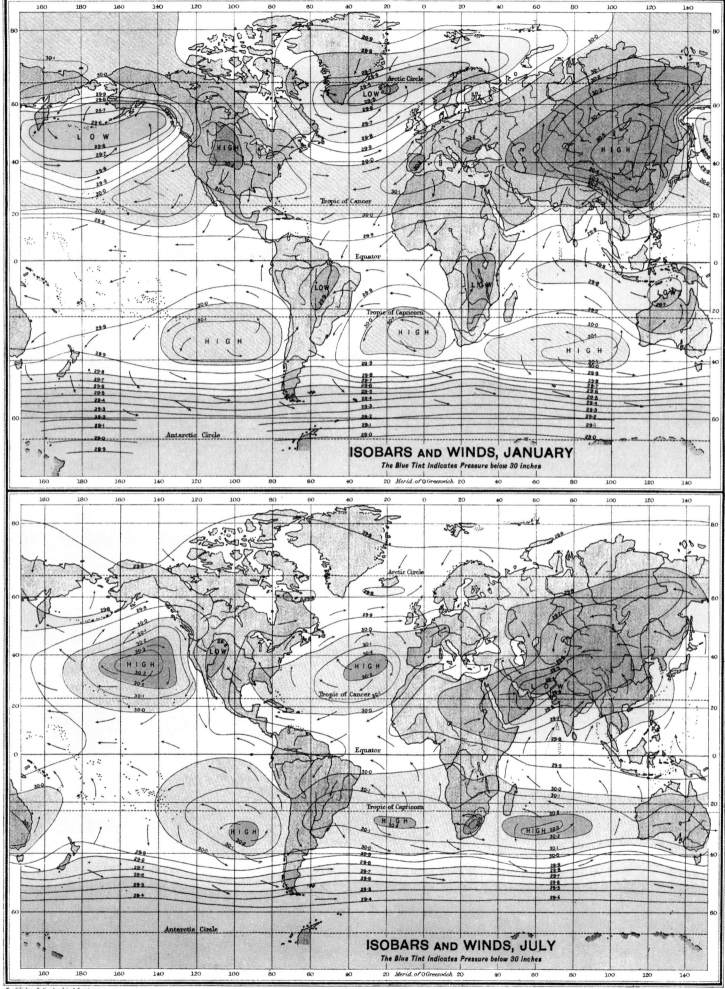

ISOBARS AND WINDS, JANUARY
The Blue Tint Indicates Pressure below 30 inches

ISOBARS AND WINDS, JULY
The Blue Tint Indicates Pressure below 30 inches

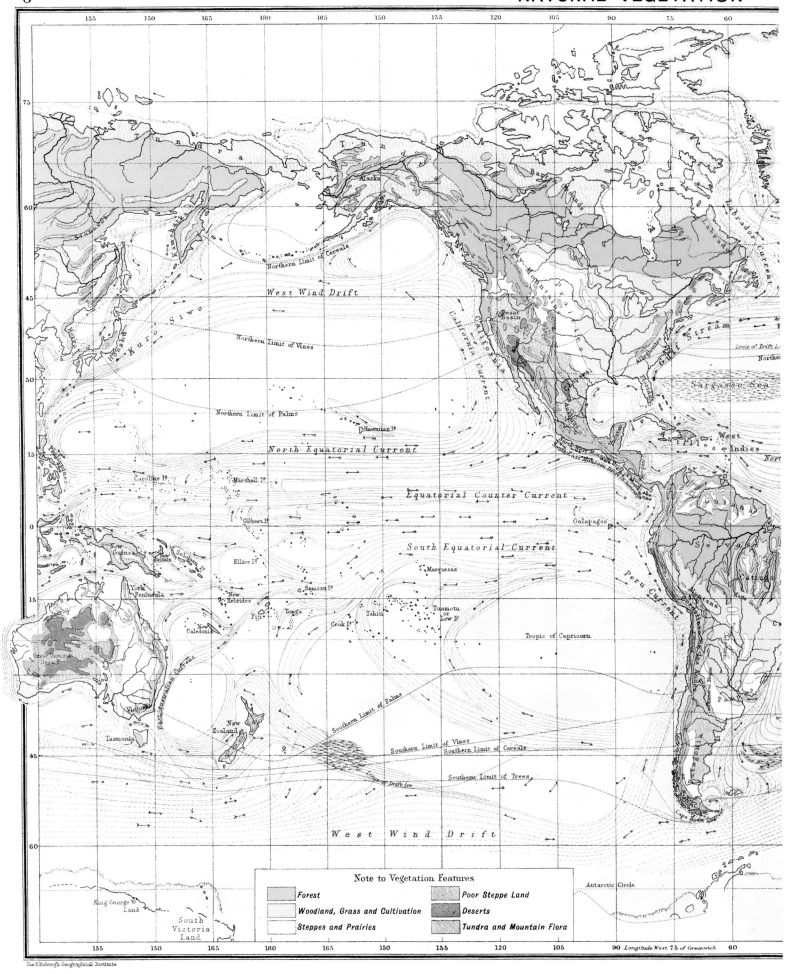

Note to Vegetation Features

Forest	Poor Steppe Land
Woodland, Grass and Cultivation	Deserts
Steppes and Prairies	Tundra and Mountain Flora

Gall's

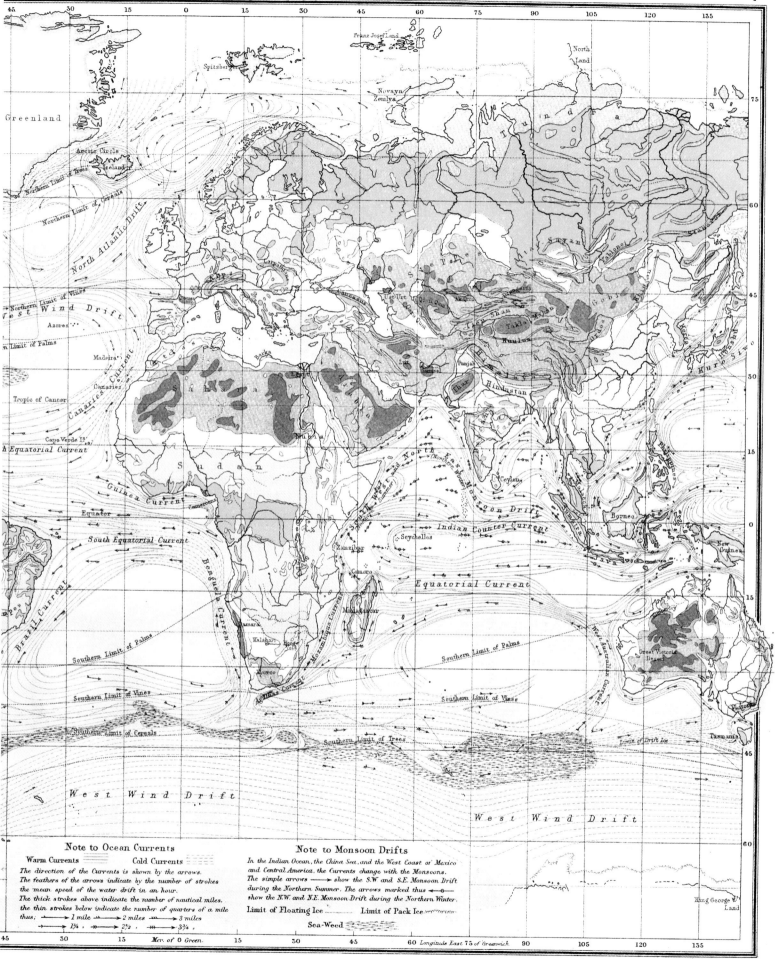

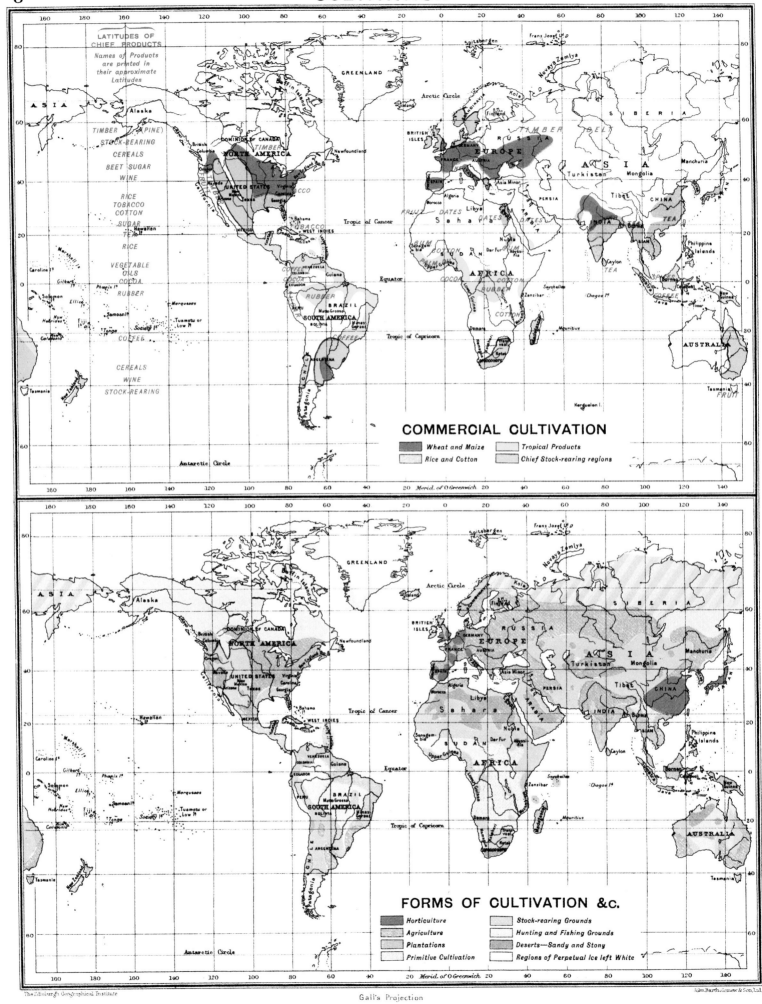

LATITUDES OF
CHIEF PRODUCTS

Names of Products
are printed in
their approximate
Latitudes

TIMBER (PINE)
STOCK-REARING
CEREALS
BEET SUGAR
WINE

RICE
TOBACCO
COTTON
SUGAR
TEA

RICE

VEGETABLE
OILS
COCOA
RUBBER

COFFEE

CEREALS
WINE
STOCK-REARING

COMMERCIAL CULTIVATION

- Wheat and Maize
- Rice and Cotton
- Tropical Products
- Chief Stock-rearing regions

FORMS OF CULTIVATION &c.

- Horticulture
- Agriculture
- Plantations
- Primitive Cultivation
- Stock-rearing Grounds
- Hunting and Fishing Grounds
- Deserts—Sandy and Stony
- Regions of Perpetual Ice left White

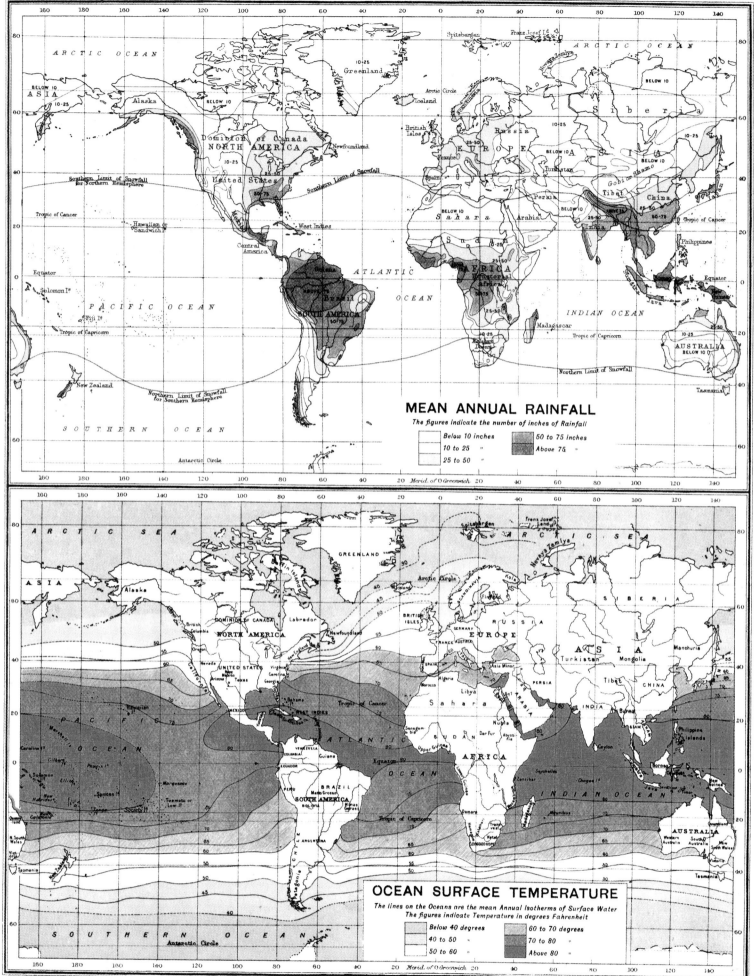

MEAN ANNUAL RAINFALL

The figures indicate the number of inches of Rainfall

Below 10 inches
10 to 25 "
25 to 50 "
50 to 75 inches
Above 75 "

OCEAN SURFACE TEMPERATURE

The lines on the Oceans are the mean Annual Isotherms of Surface Water
The figures indicate Temperature in degrees Fahrenheit

Below 40 degrees
40 to 50 "
50 to 60 "
60 to 70 degrees
70 to 80 "
Above 80 "

NOTE TO LAND COLOURING

Regions at present engaged in
International Commerce

Regions capable of Commercial Development
but at present undeveloped

Regions open to Commercial Enterprise only
during Summer Months

Barren and Desert Regions incapable of
Commercial Development

Principal Railways shown thus ————

Mercator's

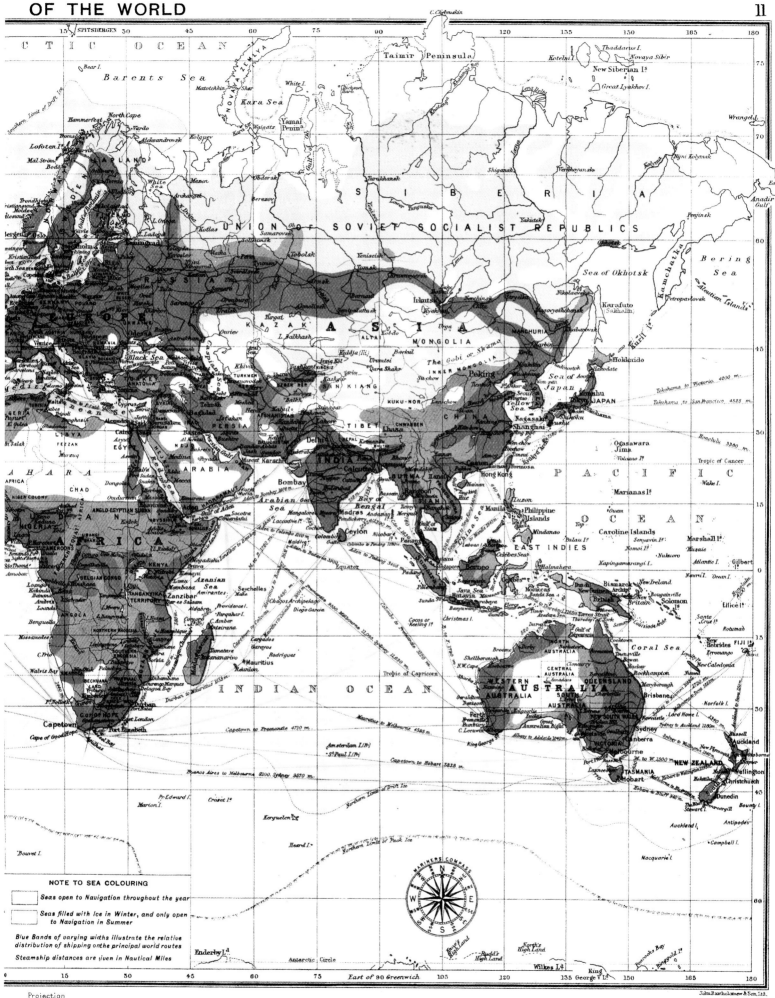

NOTE TO SEA COLOURING

Seas open to Navigation throughout the year

Seas filled with Ice in Winter, and only open
to Navigation in Summer

Blue Bands of varying widths illustrate the relative
distribution of shipping on the principal world routes

Steamship distances are given in Nautical Miles

John Bartholomew & Son, Ltd.

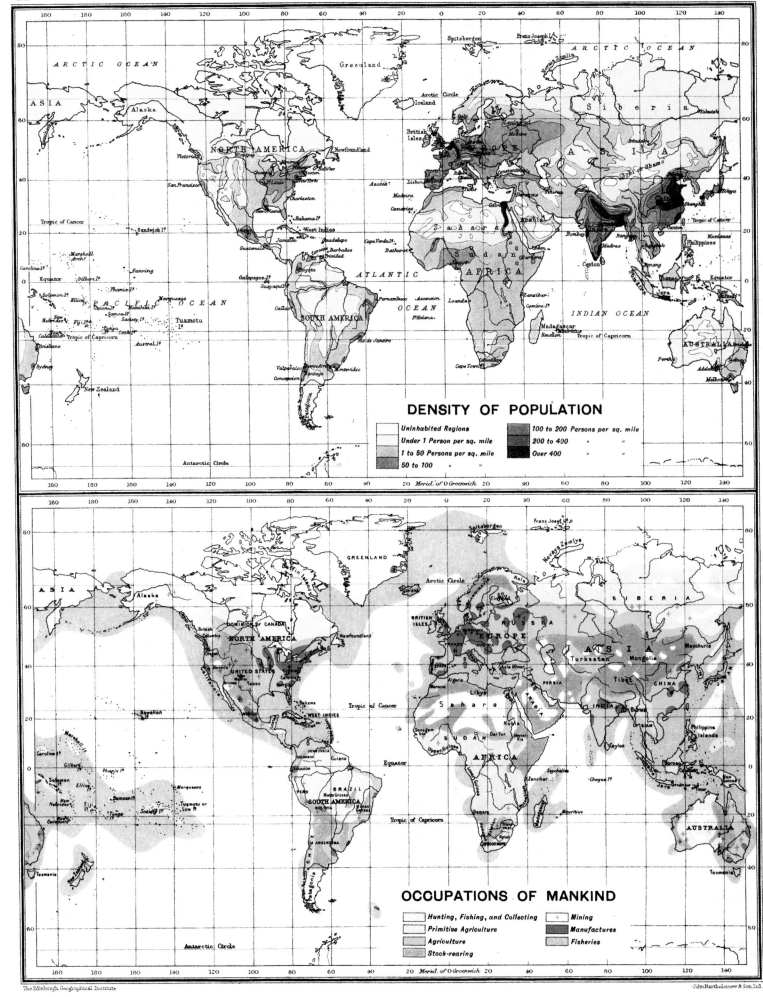

DENSITY OF POPULATION

Uninhabited Regions
Under 1 Person per sq. mile
1 to 50 Persons per sq. mile
50 to 100 "

100 to 200 Persons per sq. mile
200 to 400 "
Over 400 "

OCCUPATIONS OF MANKIND

Hunting, Fishing, and Collecting
Primitive Agriculture
Agriculture
Stock-rearing

Mining
Manufactures
Fisheries

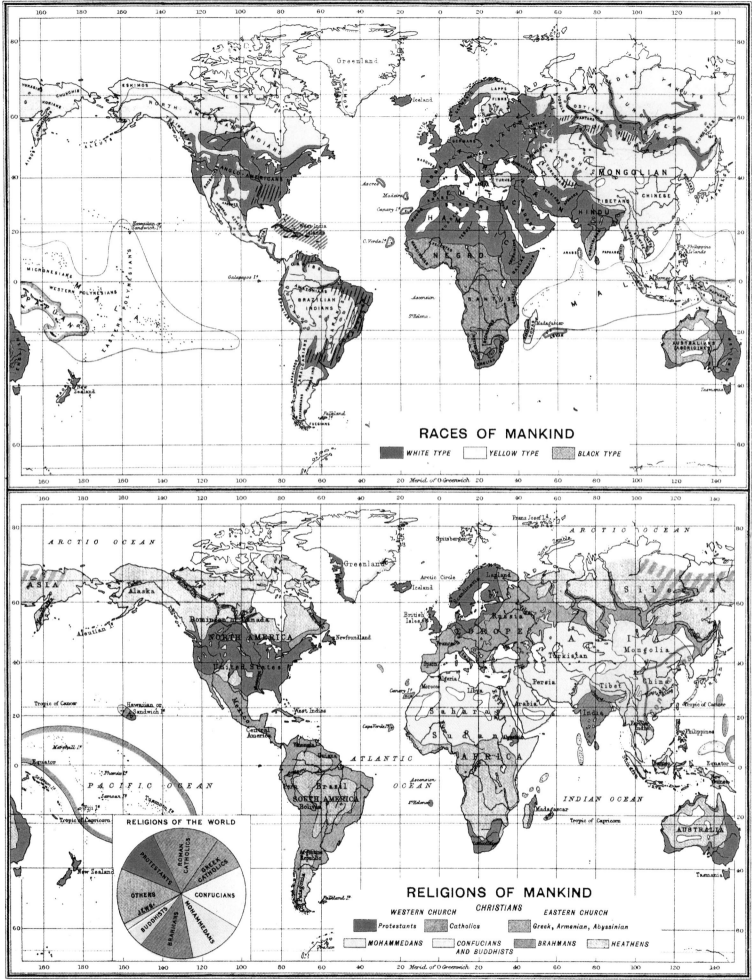

RACES OF MANKIND

WHITE TYPE YELLOW TYPE BLACK TYPE

RELIGIONS OF THE WORLD

ROMAN CATHOLICS
GREEK CATHOLICS
PROTESTANTS
CONFUCIANS
OTHERS
JEWS
MOHAMMEDANS
BUDDHISTS
BRAHMANS

RELIGIONS OF MANKIND

CHRISTIANS
WESTERN CHURCH   EASTERN CHURCH

Protestants   Catholics   Greek, Armenian, Abyssinian

MOHAMMEDANS   CONFUCIANS AND BUDDHISTS   BRAHMANS   HEATHENS

The Edinburgh Geographical Institute

Gall's Projection

John Bartholomew & Son Ltd.

Steamship distances are given in Nautical Miles

Principal Railways shown thus ———

REFERENCE T[...]
OF CHIEF W[...]

British
U.S.A.
French
Dutch

Gall's

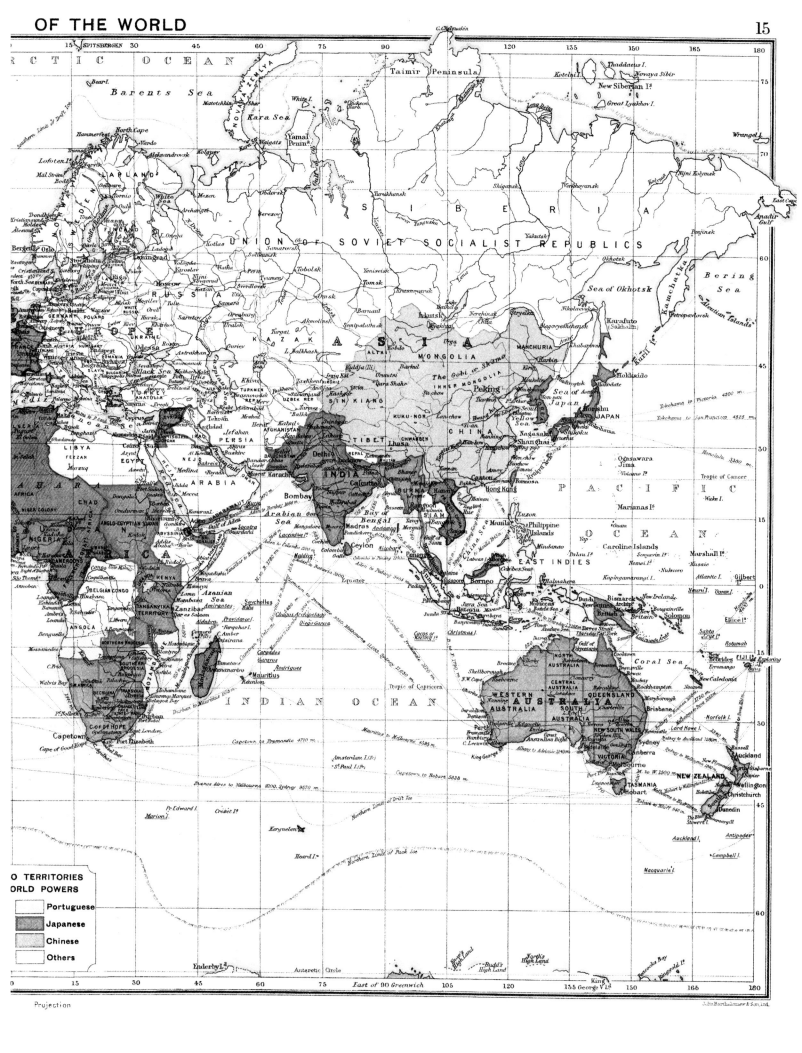

ARCTIC OCEAN

Barents Sea

Kara Sea

SIBERIA

UNION OF SOVIET SOCIALIST REPUBLICS

RUSSIA

A S I A

MONGOLIA

The Gobi or Shamo

CHINA

TIBET

INDIA

PERSIA

ARABIA

AFRICA

AUSTRALIA

INDIAN OCEAN

PACIFIC OCEAN

NEW ZEALAND

TERRITORIES
WORLD POWERS

Portuguese
Japanese
Chinese
Others

Projection   John Bartholomew & Son, Ltd.

COUNTRIES OF THE BRITISH EMPIRE
DRAWN ON A UNIFORM SCALE OF 1:60,000,000

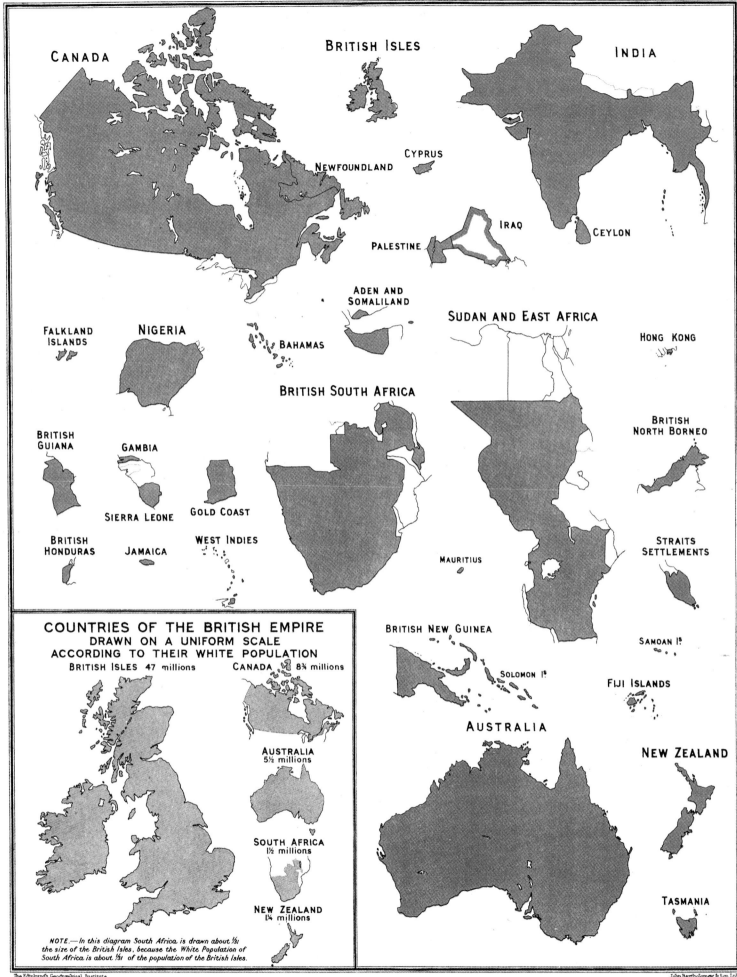

CANADA

BRITISH ISLES

INDIA

NEWFOUNDLAND

CYPRUS

IRAQ

CEYLON

PALESTINE

ADEN AND SOMALILAND

SUDAN AND EAST AFRICA

HONG KONG

FALKLAND ISLANDS

NIGERIA

BAHAMAS

BRITISH SOUTH AFRICA

BRITISH NORTH BORNEO

BRITISH GUIANA

GAMBIA

SIERRA LEONE

GOLD COAST

BRITISH HONDURAS

JAMAICA

WEST INDIES

MAURITIUS

STRAITS SETTLEMENTS

BRITISH NEW GUINEA

SAMOAN Is

SOLOMON Is

FIJI ISLANDS

AUSTRALIA

NEW ZEALAND

TASMANIA

COUNTRIES OF THE BRITISH EMPIRE
DRAWN ON A UNIFORM SCALE
ACCORDING TO THEIR WHITE POPULATION

BRITISH ISLES 47 millions

CANADA 8¾ millions

AUSTRALIA 5½ millions

SOUTH AFRICA 1½ millions

NEW ZEALAND 1¼ millions

NOTE.— In this diagram South Africa is drawn about ⅓₁ the size of the British Isles, because the White Population of South Africa is about ⅓₁ of the population of the British Isles.

The Edinburgh Geographical Institute

John Bartholomew & Son, Ltd.

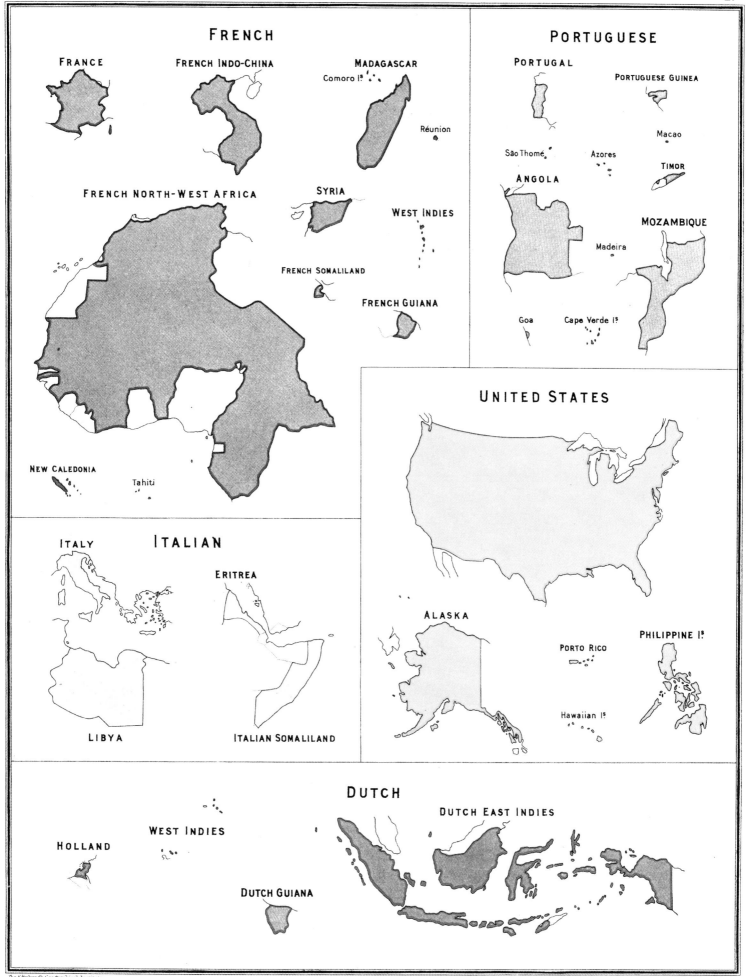

FRENCH

FRANCE

FRENCH INDO-CHINA

MADAGASCAR

Comoro Is

Réunion

FRENCH NORTH-WEST AFRICA

SYRIA

WEST INDIES

FRENCH SOMALILAND

FRENCH GUIANA

NEW CALEDONIA

Tahiti

PORTUGUESE

PORTUGAL

PORTUGUESE GUINEA

Macao

São Thomé

Azores

TIMOR

ANGOLA

MOZAMBIQUE

Madeira

Goa

Cape Verde Is

UNITED STATES

ALASKA

PORTO RICO

PHILIPPINE IS

Hawaiian Is

ITALIAN

ITALY

ERITREA

LIBYA

ITALIAN SOMALILAND

DUTCH

WEST INDIES

DUTCH EAST INDIES

HOLLAND

DUTCH GUIANA

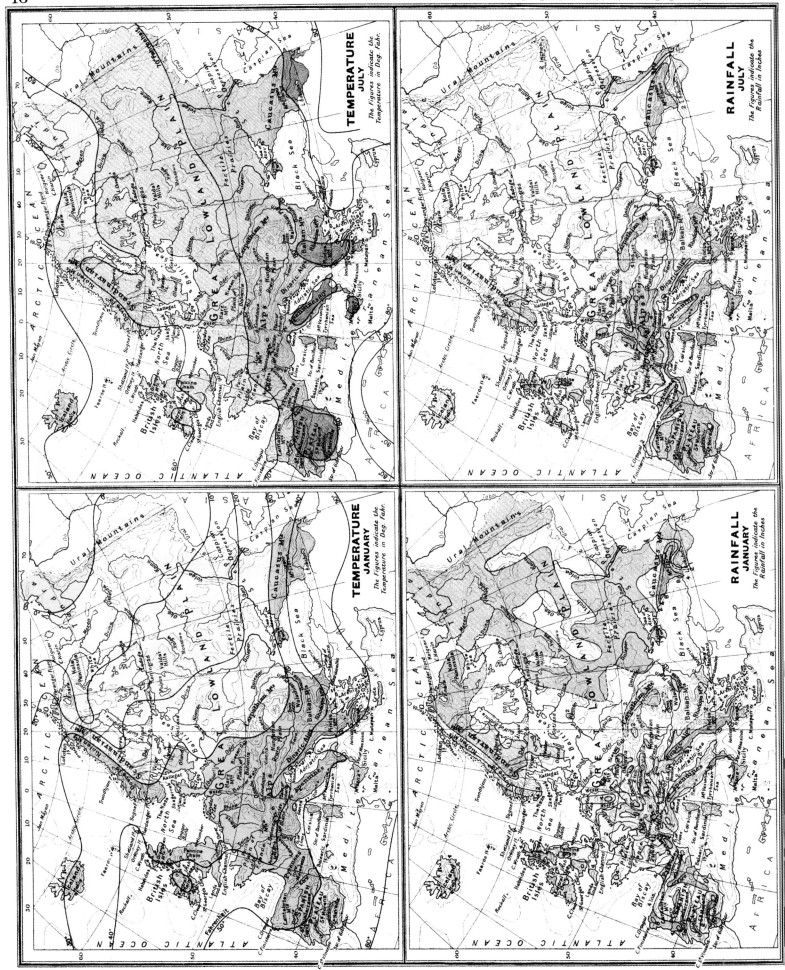

TEMPERATURE
JULY

The Figures indicate the
Temperature in Deg. Fahr.

RAINFALL
JULY

The Figures indicate the
Rainfall in Inches

TEMPERATURE
JANUARY

The Figures indicate the
Temperature in Deg. Fahr.

RAINFALL
JANUARY

The Figures indicate the
Rainfall in Inches

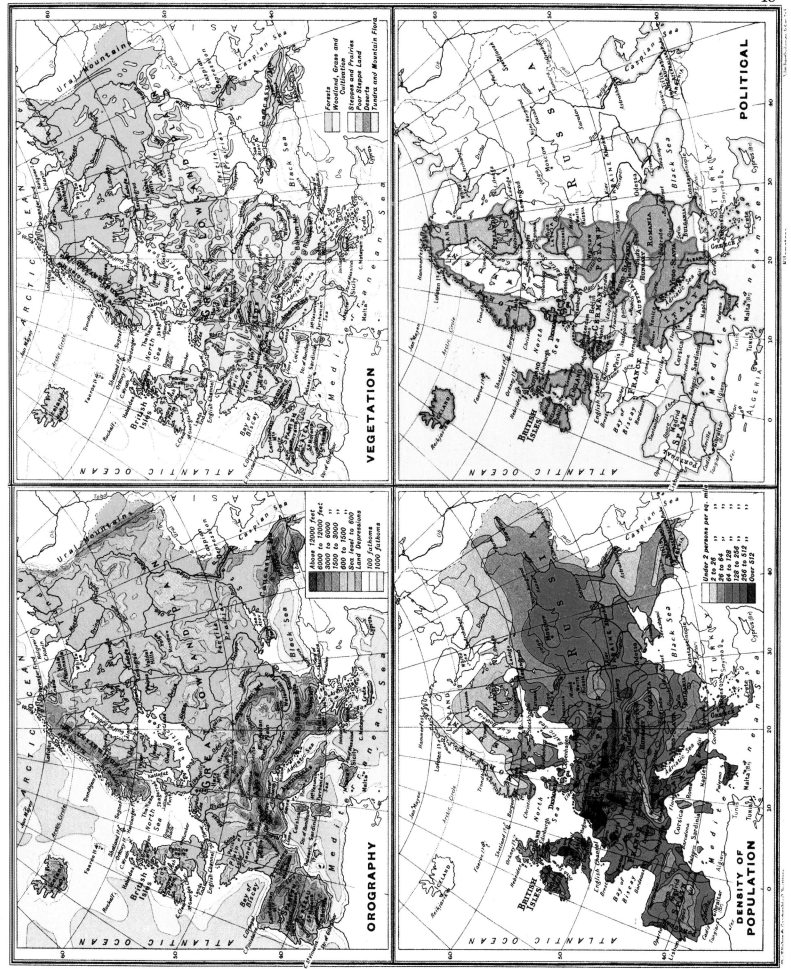

VEGETATION

POLITICAL

OROGRAPHY

DENSITY OF POPULATION

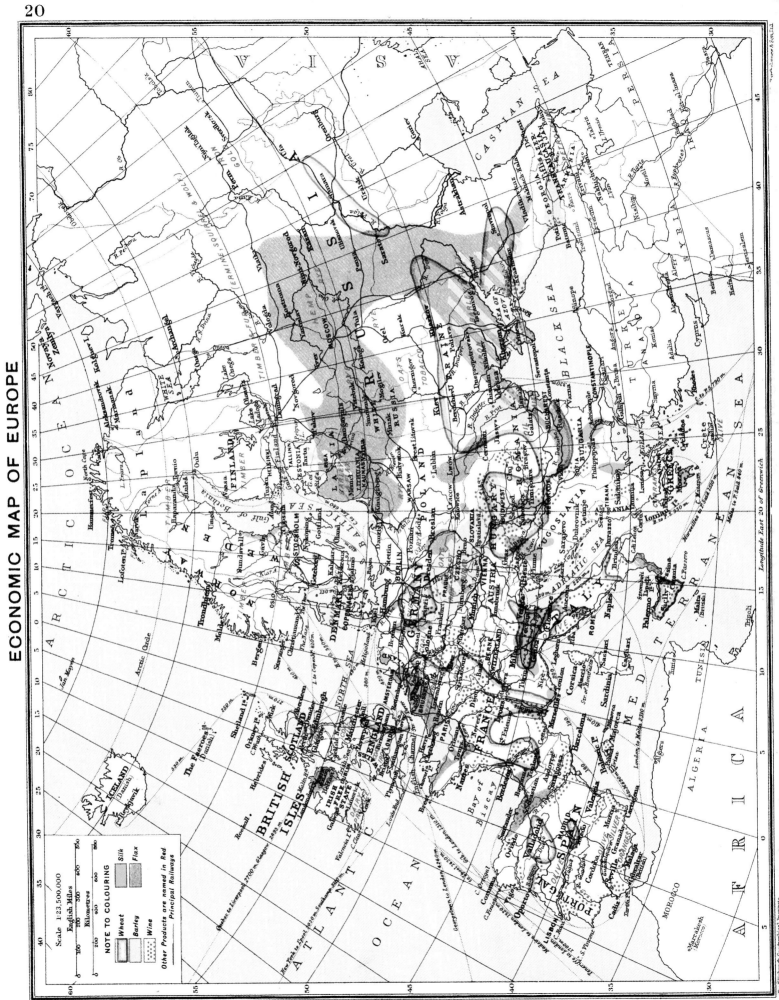

ECONOMIC MAP OF EUROPE

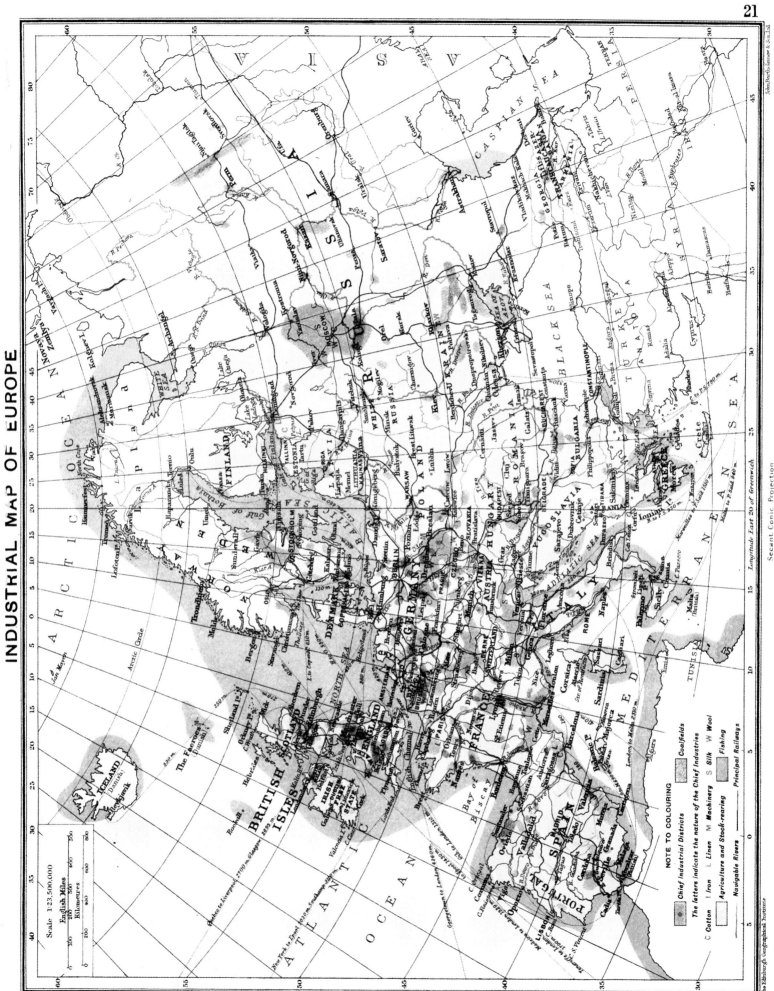

INDUSTRIAL MAP OF EUROPE

Scale 1:23,500,000

NOTE TO COLOURING

Chief Industrial Districts   Coalfields

The letters indicate the nature of the Chief Industries

C Cotton   I Iron   L Linen   M Machinery   S Silk   W Wool

     Agriculture and Stock-rearing   Fishing

Navigable Rivers   Principal Railways

Secant Conic Projection

John Bartholomew & Son, Ltd.

The Edinburgh Geographical Institute

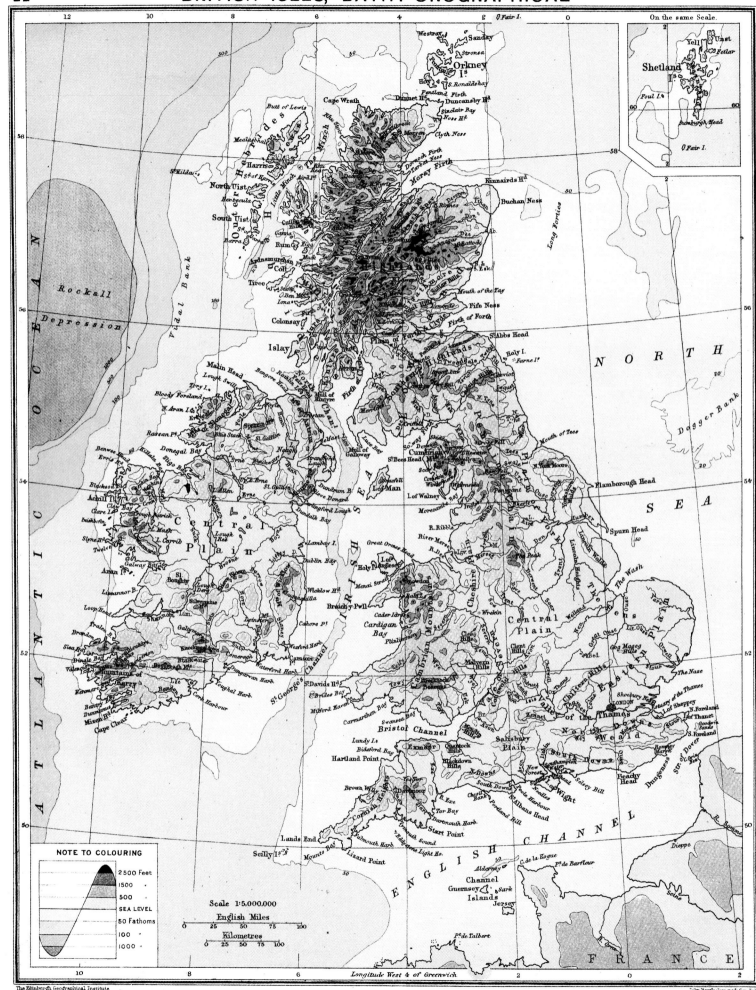

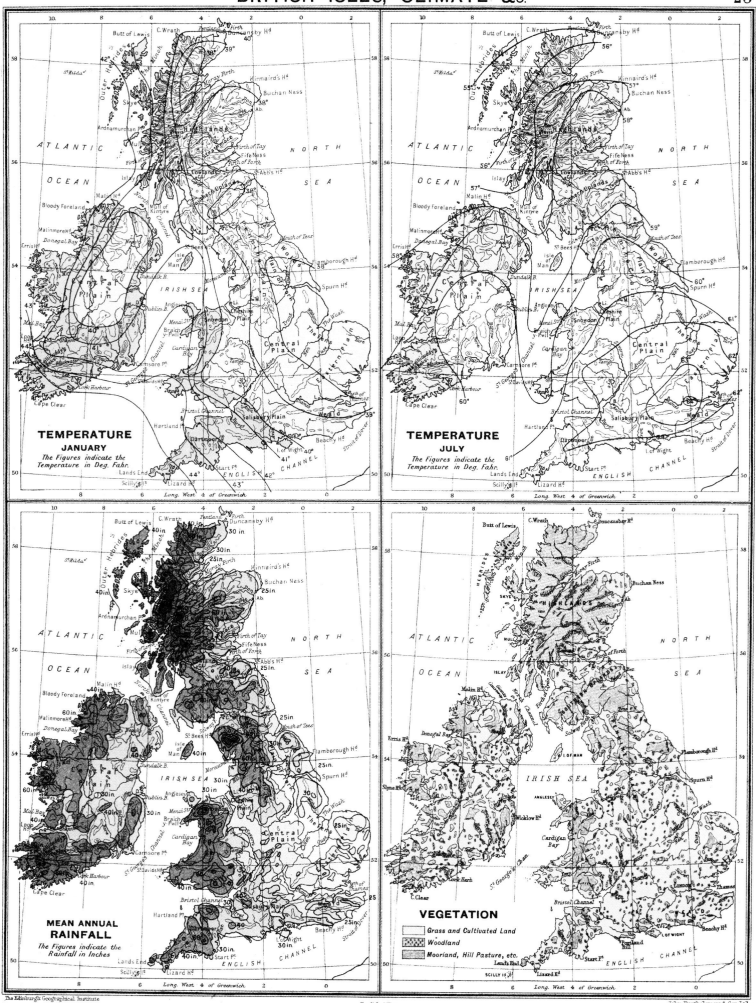

TEMPERATURE

JANUARY

The Figures indicate the Temperature in Deg. Fahr.

TEMPERATURE

JULY

The Figures indicate the Temperature in Deg. Fahr.

Long. West 4 of Greenwich

MEAN ANNUAL RAINFALL

The Figures indicate the Rainfall in Inches

VEGETATION

Grass and Cultivated Land
Woodland
Moorland, Hill Pasture, etc.

Long. West 4 of Greenwich

The Edinburgh Geographical Institute

John Bartholomew & Son, Ltd.

English Miles

0   50   100   150   200   250

Scale 1:5,300,000

English Miles

Kilomètres

NOTE TO COLOURING

Uninhabited Regions
1 to 64 Persons per square mile
64 to 128 "
128 to 256 "
256 to 512 "
Over 512 "

Towns of 10,000 inhabitants and
upwards are shown according to
population, and are excluded from
density calculations.

■ Towns over 200,000 inhabitants
■ " 100,000 "
● " 50,000 "
● " 10,000 "

Principal Railways shown thus

John Bartholomew & Son, Ltd.

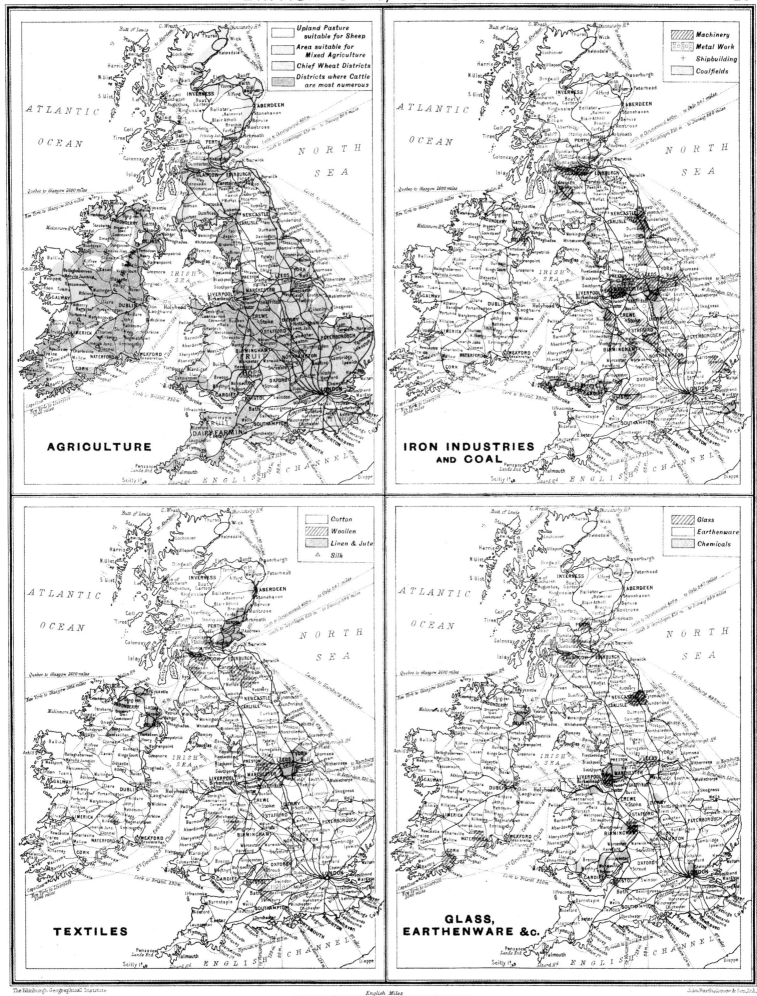

AGRICULTURE

Upland Pasture suitable for Sheep
Area suitable for Mixed Agriculture
Chief Wheat Districts
Districts where Cattle are most numerous

IRON INDUSTRIES and COAL

Machinery
Metal Work
Shipbuilding
Coalfields

TEXTILES

Cotton
Woollen
Linen & Jute
Silk

GLASS, EARTHENWARE &c.

Glass
Earthenware
Chemicals

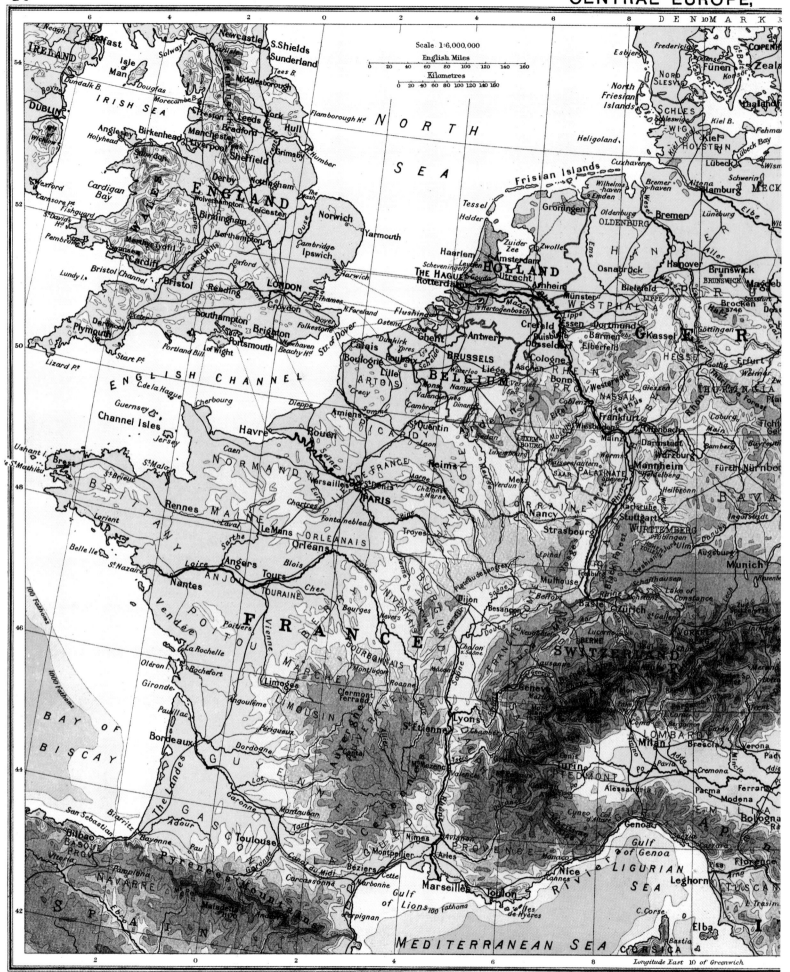

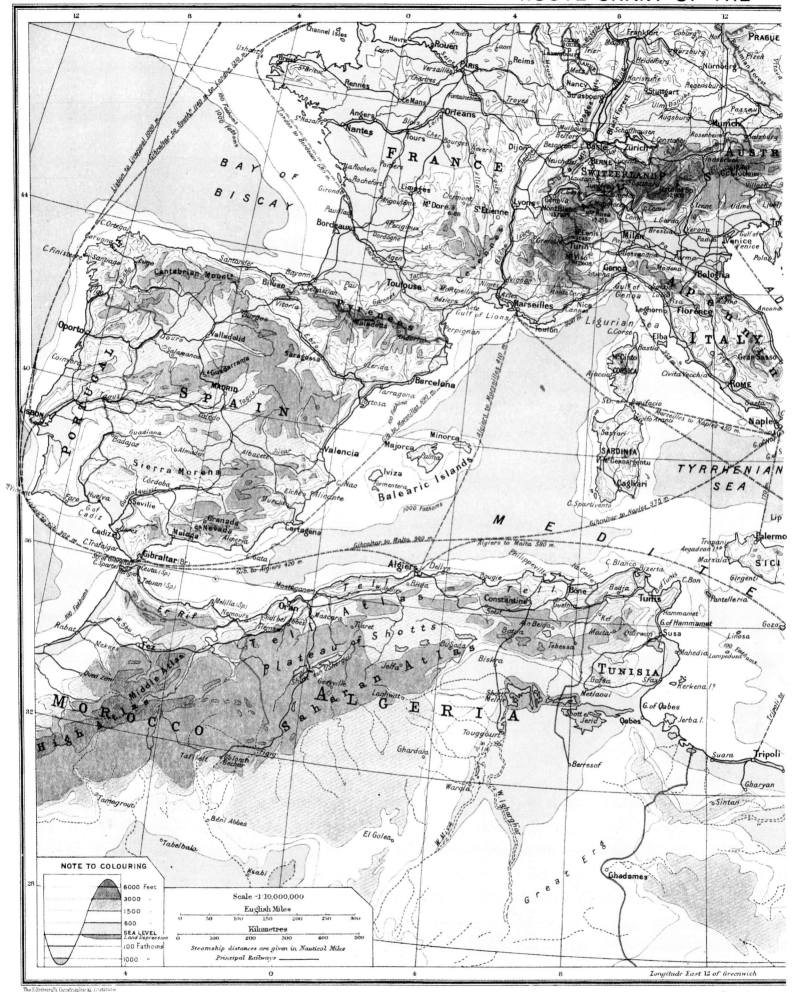

NOTE TO COLOURING

6000 Feet
3000
1500
600
SEA LEVEL
Land Depression
100 Fathoms
1000 "

Scale 1:10,000,000
English Miles
0   50   100   150   200   250   300
Kilometres
0   100   200   300   400   500
Steamship distances are given in Nautical Miles
Principal Railways _____

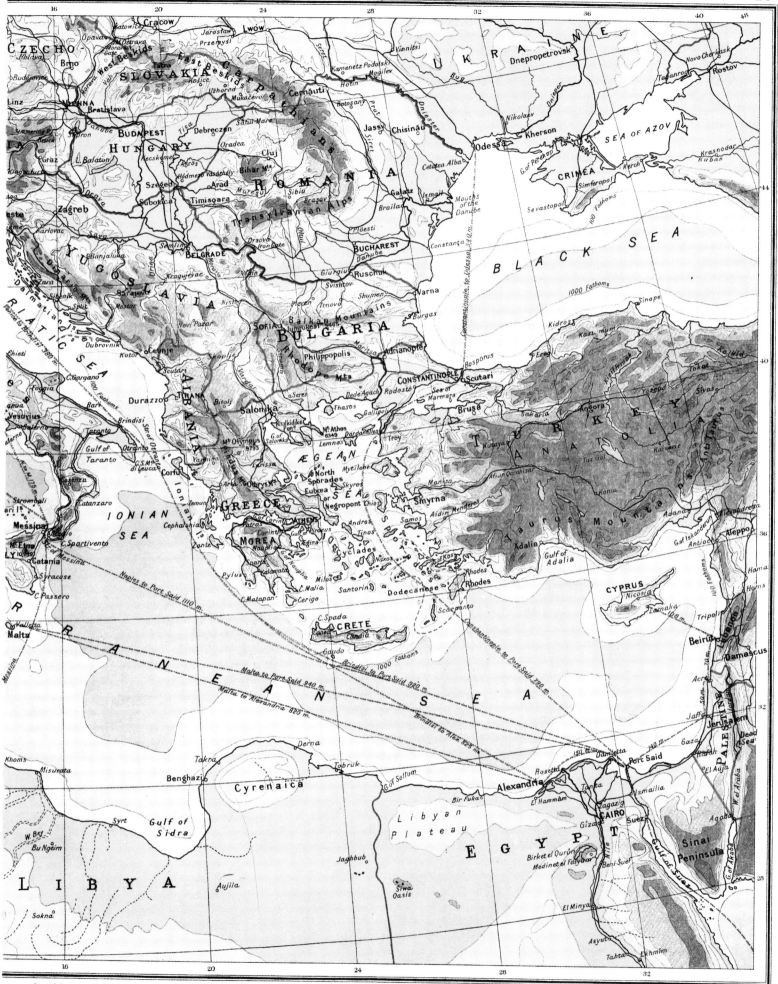

TRADE ROUTES BETWEEN EUROPE AND ASIA

Trade Routes are shown in red
— Railways open
— — Constructing
— Navigable Rivers
Steamship distances are given in Nautical miles
British Possessions coloured red

Mercator's Projection

John Bartholomew & Son, Ltd.

The Edinburgh Geographical Institute

Longitude East 60 of Greenwich

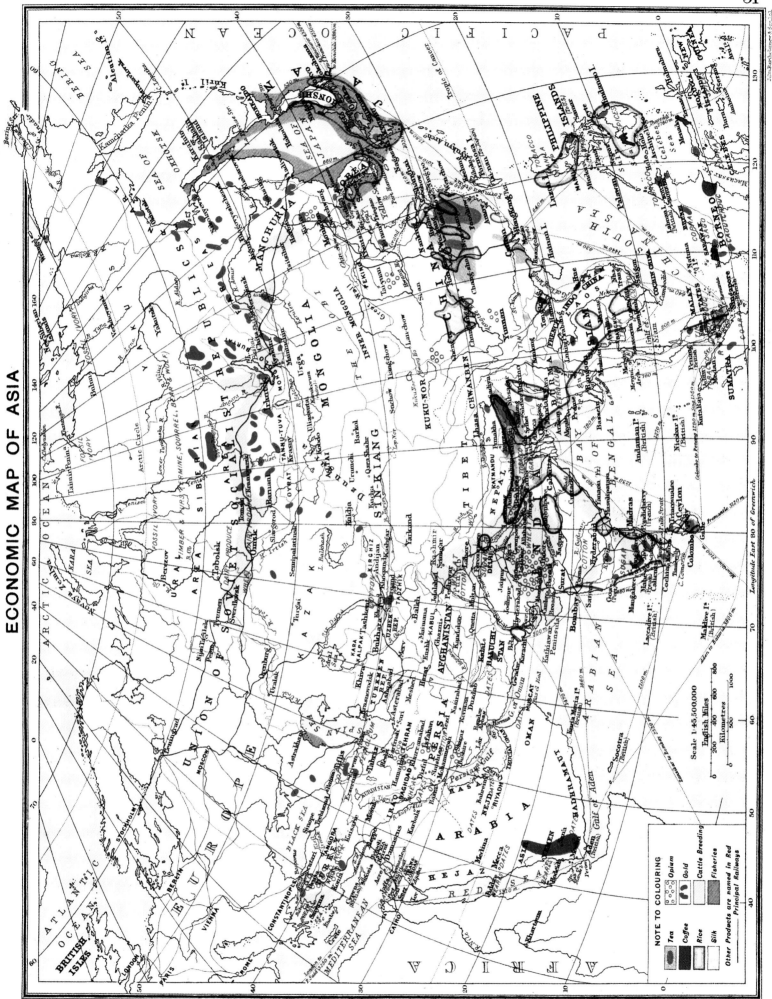

ECONOMIC MAP OF ASIA

Scale 1:45,500,000

English Miles
200   400   600   800

Kilometres
500   1000

NOTE TO COLOURING

Tea	Opium
Coffee	Gold
Rice	Cattle Breeding
Silk	Fisheries

Other Products are named in Red
— Principal Railways

John Bartholomew & Son, Ltd.

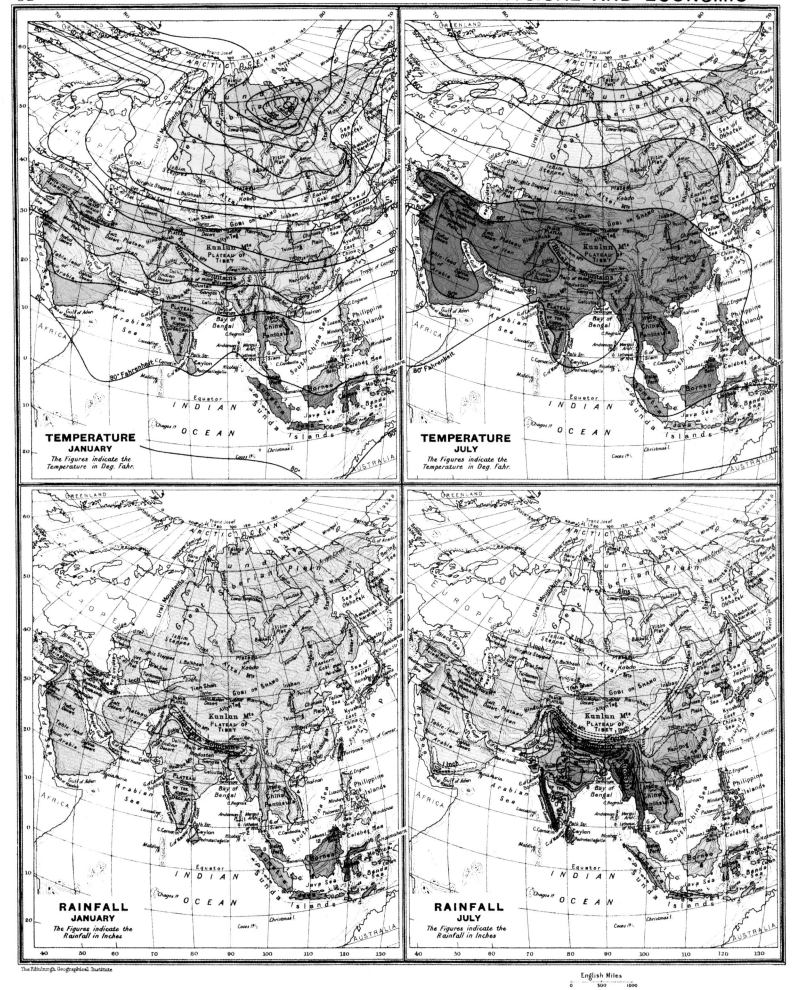

TEMPERATURE
JANUARY
*The Figures indicate the
Temperature in Deg. Fahr.*

TEMPERATURE
JULY
*The Figures indicate the
Temperature in Deg. Fahr.*

RAINFALL
JANUARY
*The Figures indicate the
Rainfall in Inches*

RAINFALL
JULY
*The Figures indicate the
Rainfall in Inches*

The Edinburgh Geographical Institute

English Miles
0   500   1000

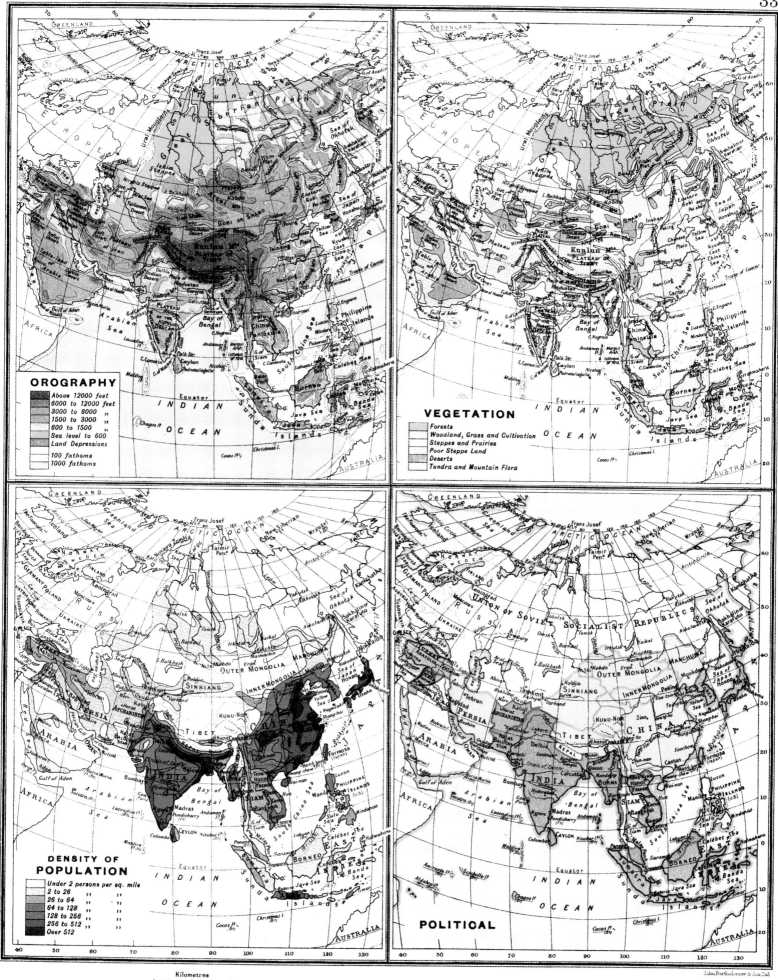

OROGRAPHY

- Above 12000 feet
- 6000 to 12000 feet
- 3000 to 6000 "
- 1500 to 3000 "
- 600 to 1500 "
- Sea level to 600
- Land Depressions
- 100 fathoms
- 1000 fathoms

VEGETATION

- Forests
- Woodland, Grass and Cultivation
- Steppes and Prairies
- Poor Steppe Land
- Deserts
- Tundra and Mountain Flora

DENSITY OF POPULATION

- Under 2 persons per sq. mile
- 2 to 26 " "
- 26 to 64 " "
- 64 to 128 " "
- 128 to 256 " "
- 256 to 512 " "
- Over 512

POLITICAL

Kilometres

0   1000   2000

John Bartholomew & Son, Ltd.

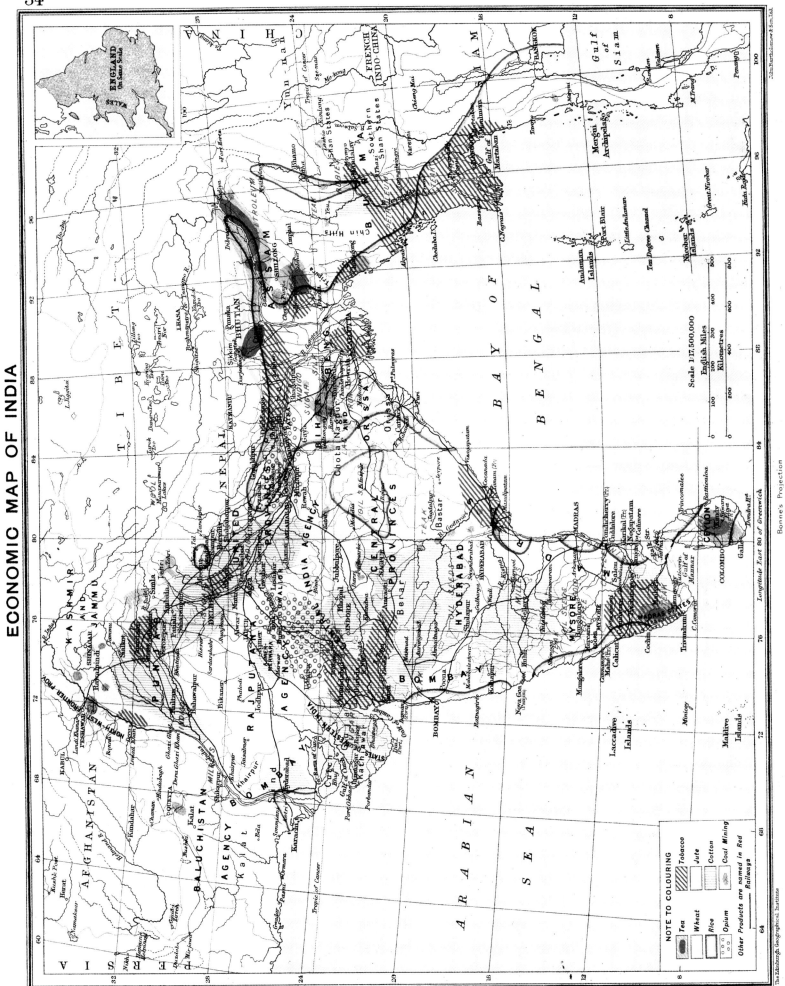

ECONOMIC MAP OF INDIA

34

ECONOMIC MAP OF THE FAR EAST

NOTE TO COLOURING

Tea		Silk	
Rice		Wheat	

Sorghums and Millets

Other Products are named in Red

Railways

Scale 1:15,000,000

English Miles

Kilometres

Bonne's Projection

The Edinburgh Geographical Institute

MANCHURIA

MONGOLIA

INNER MONGOLIA

CHAHAR

SUIYUAN

GOBI OR SHAMO

NINGHSIA

KANSU

SHENSI

SHANSI

HONAN

HUPEH

HUNAN

KWEICHOW

KWANGSI

KWANGTUNG

SZECHWAN

CHINA

JAPAN

HOKKAIDO

HONSHIU

SHIKOKU

KIUSHIU

KOREA or CHOSEN

FORMOSA OR TAIWAN

HAINAN

PACIFIC OCEAN

SEA OF JAPAN

YELLOW SEA or HWANG HAI

TUNG HAI OR EASTERN SEA

KOREA STRAIT

FORMOSA STRAIT

GULF OF TONGKING

Tropic of Cancer

Longitude East of Greenwich

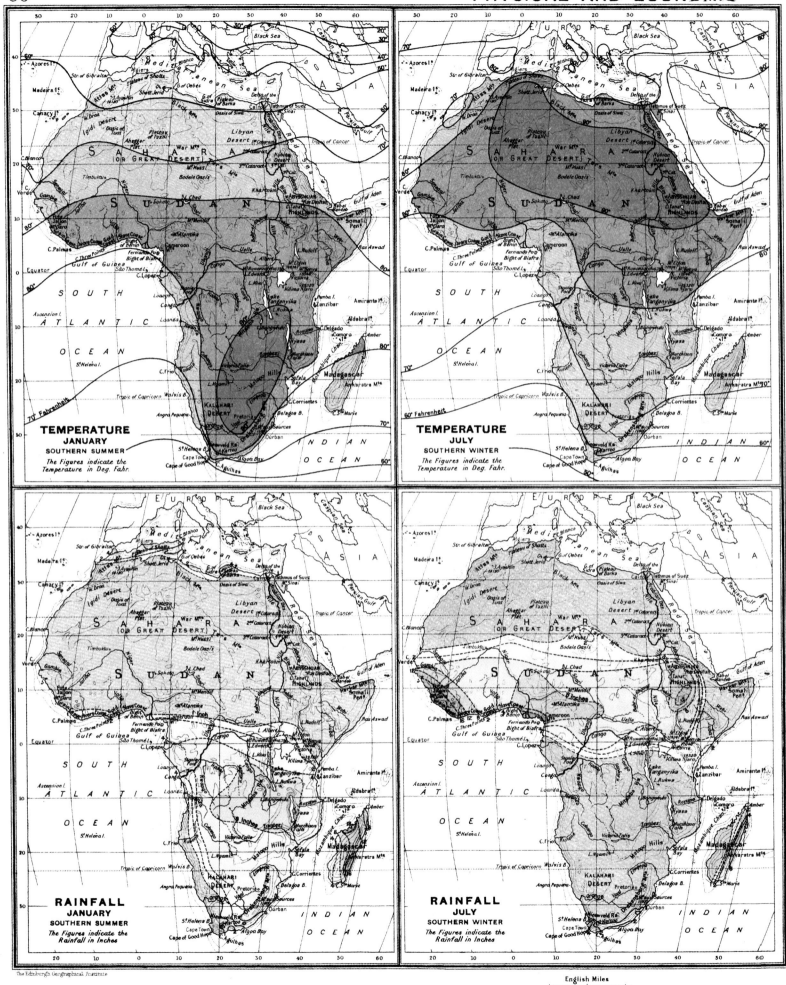

TEMPERATURE
JANUARY
SOUTHERN SUMMER
The Figures indicate the
Temperature in Deg. Fahr.

TEMPERATURE
JULY
SOUTHERN WINTER
The Figures indicate the
Temperature in Deg. Fahr.

RAINFALL
JANUARY
SOUTHERN SUMMER
The Figures indicate the
Rainfall in Inches

RAINFALL
JULY
SOUTHERN WINTER
The Figures indicate the
Rainfall in Inches

The Edinburgh Geographical Institute

English Miles
0   500   1000

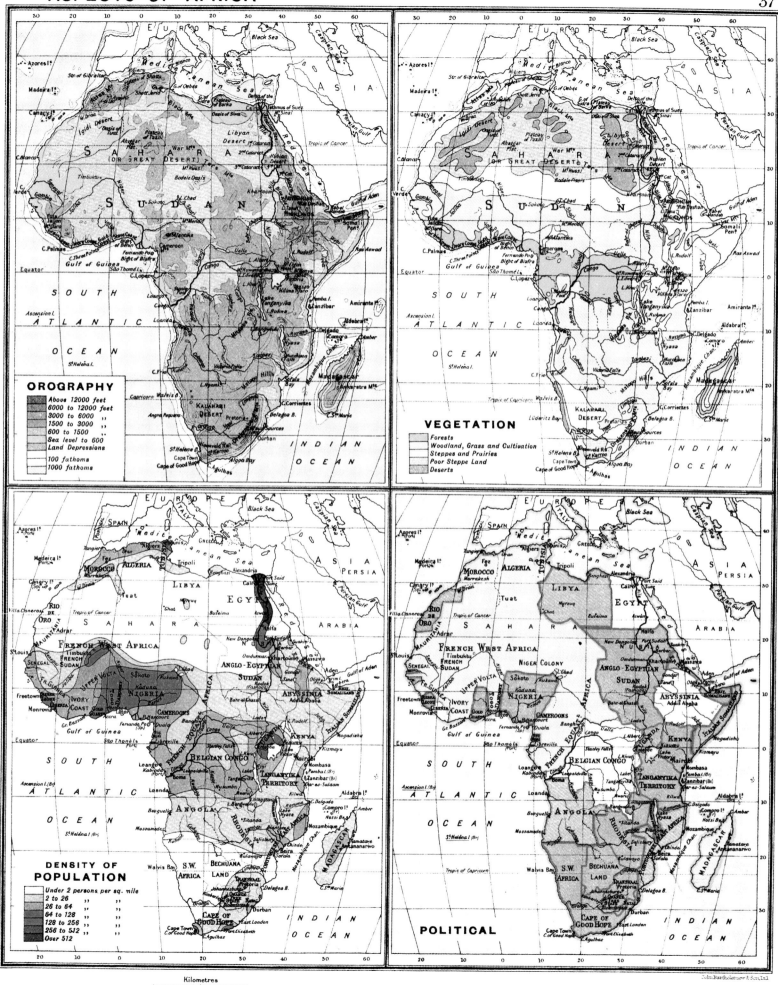

OROGRAPHY

- Above 12000 feet
- 6000 to 12000 feet
- 3000 to 6000 ,,
- 1500 to 3000 ,,
- 600 to 1500 ,,
- Sea level to 600
- Land Depressions
- 100 fathoms
- 1000 fathoms

VEGETATION

- Forests
- Woodland, Grass and Cultivation
- Steppes and Prairies
- Poor Steppe Land
- Deserts

DENSITY OF POPULATION

- Under 2 persons per sq. mile
- 2 to 26 ,, ,,
- 26 to 64 ,, ,,
- 64 to 128 ,, ,,
- 128 to 256 ,, ,,
- 256 to 512 ,, ,,
- Over 512

POLITICAL

Kilometres
0   1000   2000

John Bartholomew & Son, Ltd.

ECONOMIC MAP OF AFRICA

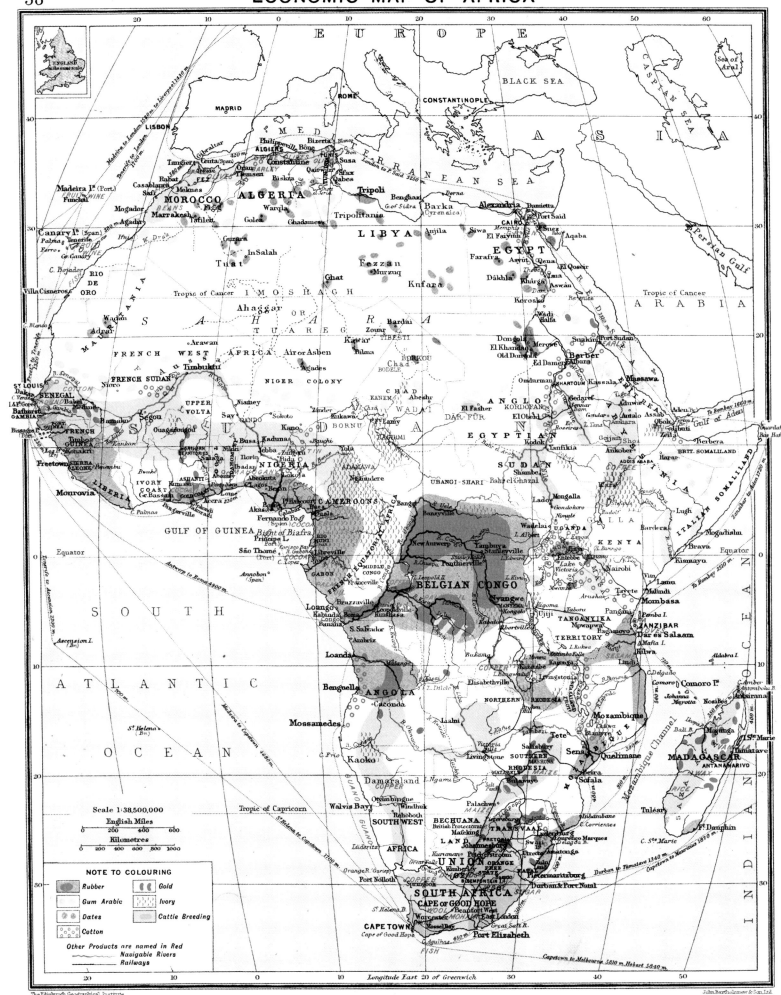

NOTE TO COLOURING

- Rubber
- Gum Arabic
- Dates
- Cotton
- Gold
- Ivory
- Cattle Breeding

Other Products are named in Red
Navigable Rivers
Railways

Scale 1:38,500,000

English Miles
0   200   400   600

Kilometres
0   200   400   600   800   1000

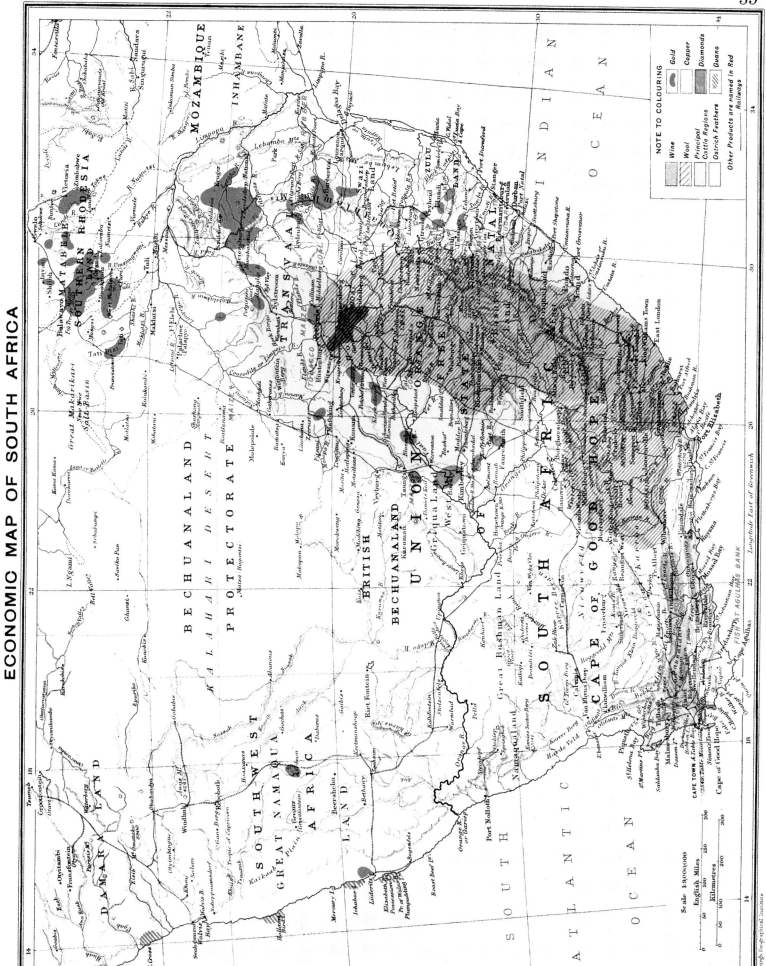

ECONOMIC MAP OF SOUTH AFRICA

39

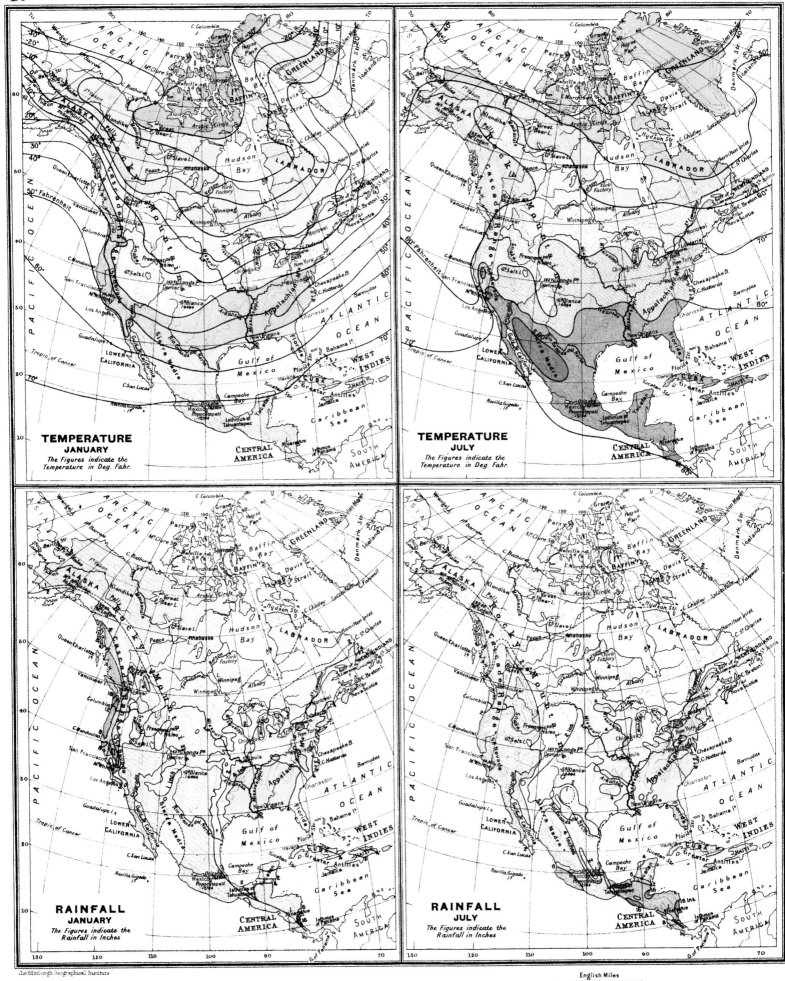

TEMPERATURE
JANUARY
The Figures indicate the
Temperature in Deg. Fahr.

TEMPERATURE
JULY
The Figures indicate the
Temperature in Deg. Fahr.

RAINFALL
JANUARY
The Figures indicate the
Rainfall in Inches

RAINFALL
JULY
The Figures indicate the
Rainfall in Inches

The Edinburgh Geographical Institute

English Miles
0   500   1000

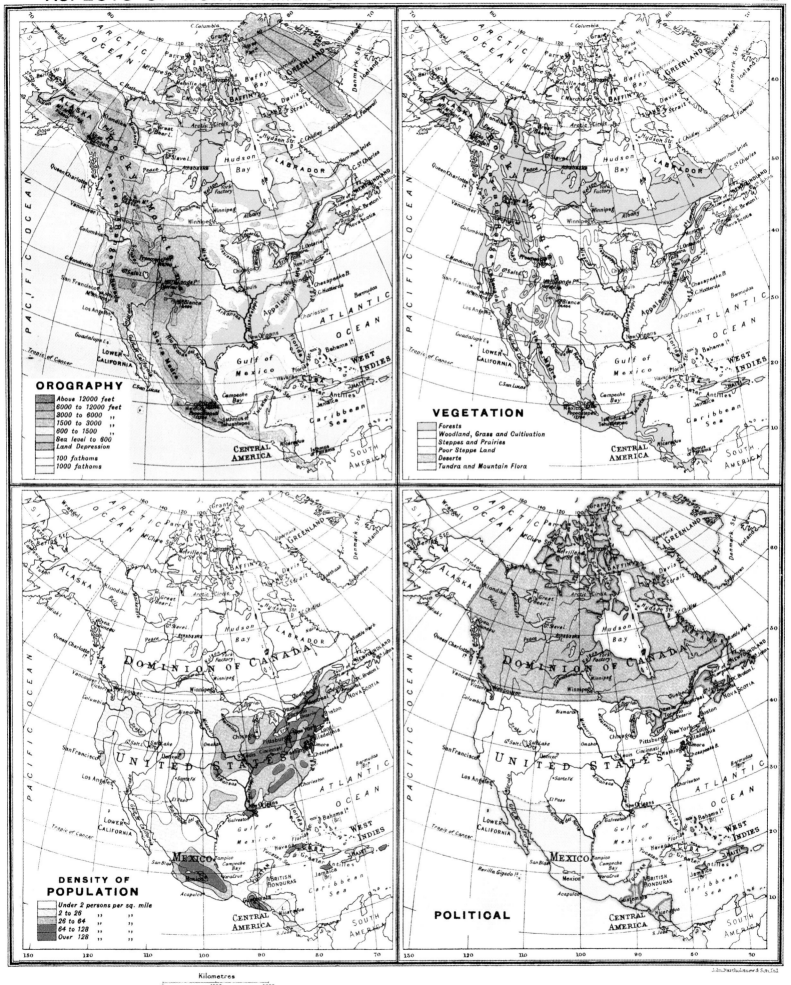

OROGRAPHY

- Above 12000 feet
- 6000 to 12000 feet
- 3000 to 6000 "
- 1500 to 3000 "
- 600 to 1500 "
- Sea level to 600
- Land Depression
- 100 fathoms
- 1000 fathoms

VEGETATION

- Forests
- Woodland, Grass and Cultivation
- Steppes and Prairies
- Poor Steppe Land
- Deserte
- Tundra and Mountain Flora

DENSITY OF POPULATION

- Under 2 persons per sq. mile
- 2 to 26 " "
- 26 to 64 " "
- 64 to 128 " "
- Over 128 " "

POLITICAL

Kilometres

0   1000   2000

John Bartholomew & Son, Ltd.

NOTE TO COLOURING

Chief Manufacturing Districts

The Letters at the Manufacturing Districts
Indicate the nature of the Chief Industries

C Cotton   I Iron Ware and Machinery
Le Leather   S Silk   Su Sugar   W Wool

Agriculture   Mining
Live Stock   Fishing

Navigable Rivers
Principal Railways

Scale 1:33,500,000
English Miles
Kilometres

The Edinburgh Geographical Institute

Bonne's Projection

John Bartholomew & Son, Ltd.

ECONOMIC MAP OF UNITED STATES AND CANADA

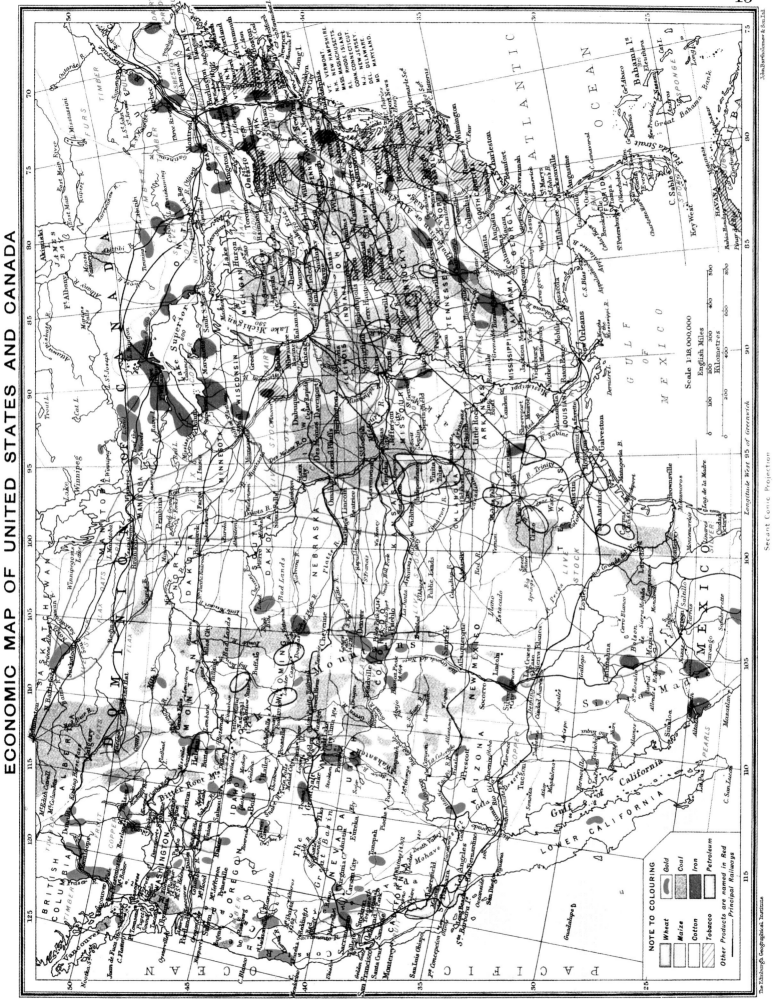

Scale 1:18,000,000

English Miles

Kilometres

Longitude West 95 of Greenwich

Secant Conic Projection

John Bartholomew & Son, Ltd.

The Edinburgh Geographical Institute

NOTE TO COLOURING

Wheat
Maize
Cotton
Tobacco

Gold
Coal
Iron
Petroleum

Other Products are named in Red
Principal Railways

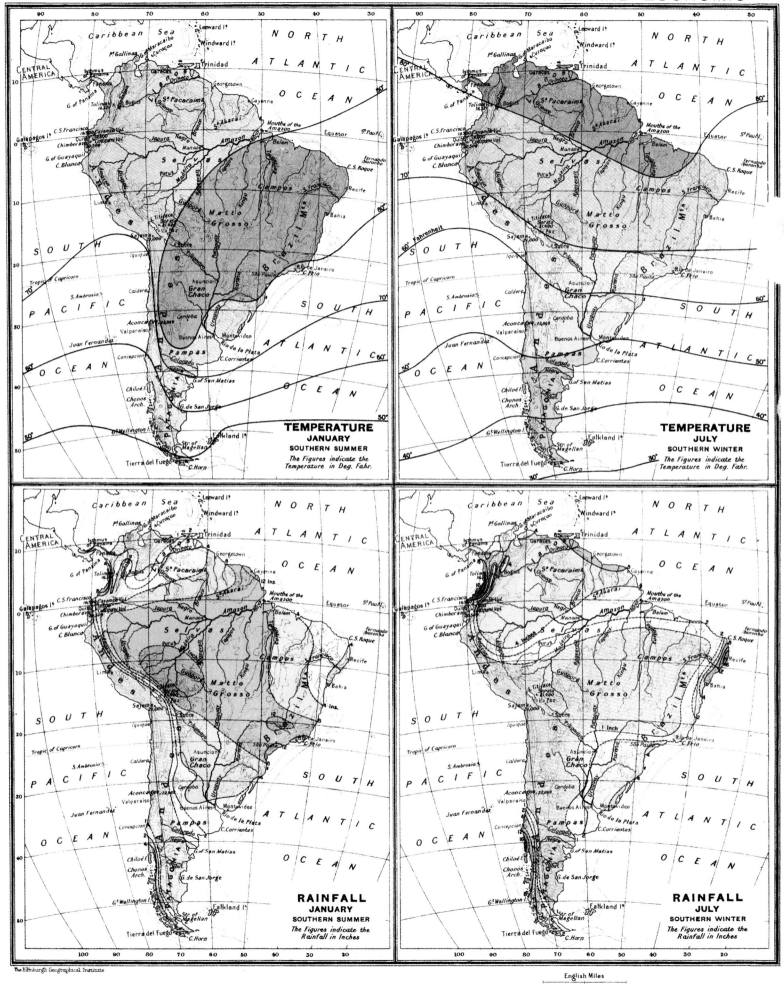

TEMPERATURE
JANUARY
SOUTHERN SUMMER
The Figures indicate the
Temperature in Deg. Fahr.

TEMPERATURE
JULY
SOUTHERN WINTER
The Figures indicate the
Temperature in Deg. Fahr.

RAINFALL
JANUARY
SOUTHERN SUMMER
The Figures indicate the
Rainfall in Inches

RAINFALL
JULY
SOUTHERN WINTER
The Figures indicate the
Rainfall in Inches

English Miles

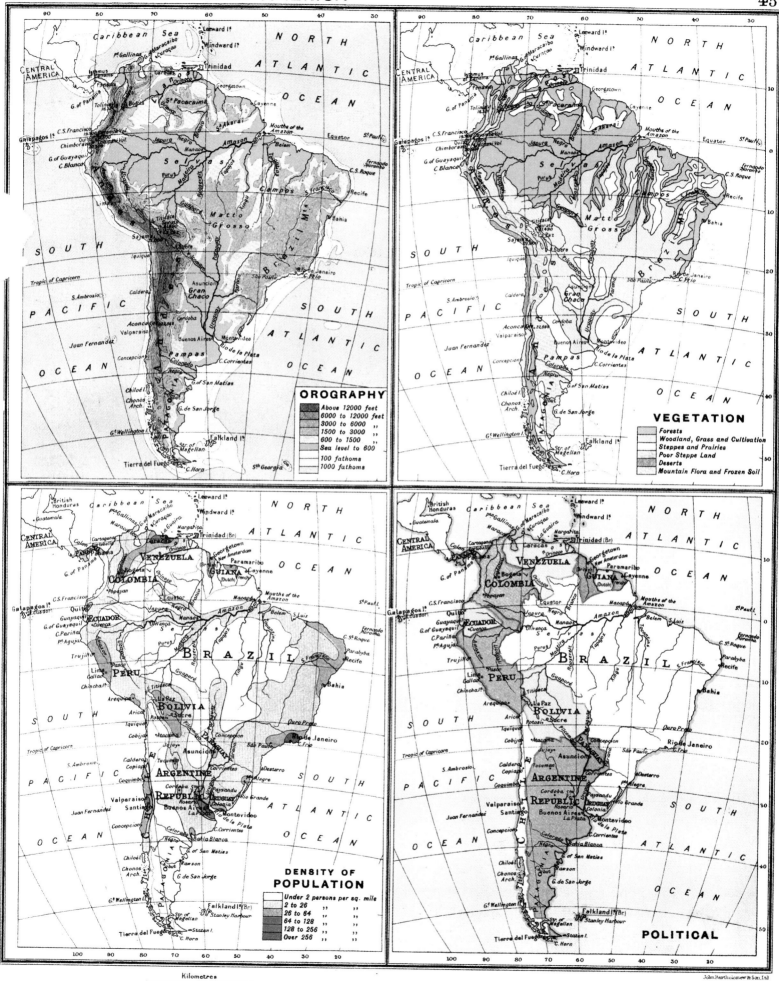

OROGRAPHY

Above 12000 feet
6000 to 12000 feet
3000 to 6000 „
1500 to 3000 „
600 to 1500 „
Sea level to 600 „
100 fathoms
1000 fathoms

VEGETATION

Forests
Woodland, Grass and Cultivation
Steppes and Prairies
Poor Steppe Land
Deserts
Mountain Flora and Frozen Soil

DENSITY OF POPULATION

Under 2 persons per sq. mile
2 to 26   „   „
26 to 64   „   „
64 to 128   „   „
128 to 256   „   „
Over 256   „   „

POLITICAL

Kilometres

0   1000   2000

John Bartholomew & Son, Ltd.

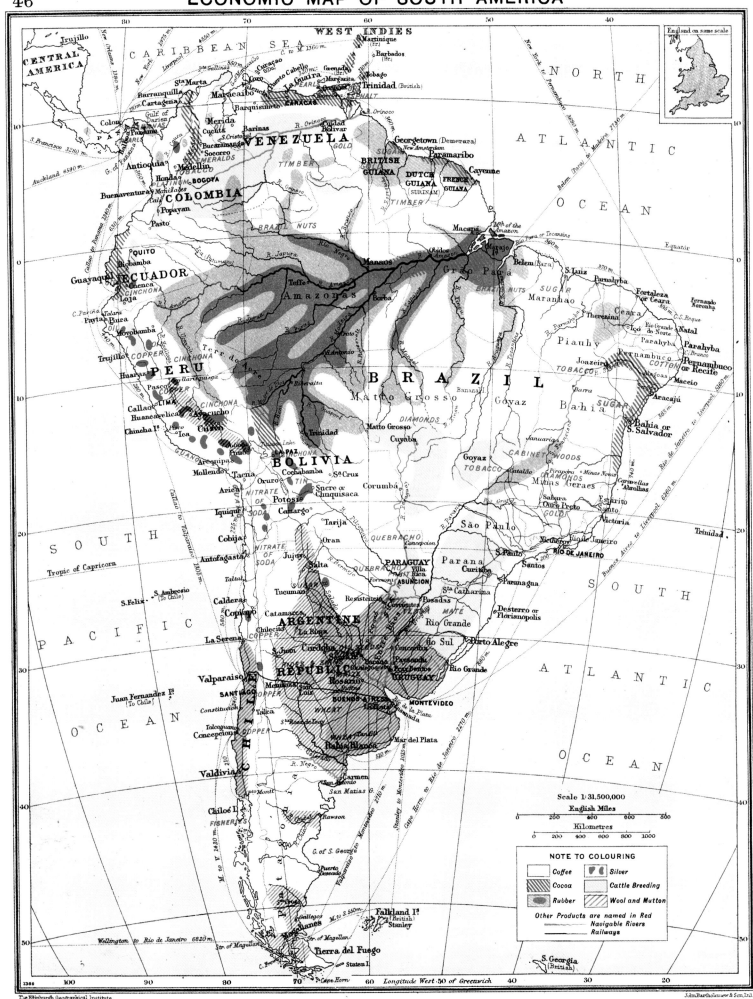

NOTE TO COLOURING

	Coffee		Silver
	Cocoa		Cattle Breeding
	Rubber		Wool and Mutton

Other Products are named in Red
Navigable Rivers
Railways

Scale 1:31,500,000
English Miles
Kilometres

England on same scale

ECONOMIC MAP OF AUSTRALASIA

England on same scale

BORNEO

CELEBES
SPICES
COFFEE
Macassar
Boni G.
Saleyer
Sumbawa
Lombok
Flores
Savu
Timor
TEAK
Sandalwood
SANDALWOOD
COFFEE
Sumba
Rotti

Banda Sea
Buru
TREPANG
Ombaya
Wetter
Letti Is.
TREPANG
Arafura Sea
Timor Sea
Kei Is.
Timorlaut Is.
Wessel Is.

NEW GUINEA
Papua
SAGO
Dutch Terr.
New Britain
New Guinea

Solomon Islands
Buka
Bougainville
Choiseul
New Georgia
Isabel
Malaita
San Christoval
Guadalcanar
Rennell

New Hebrides
Banks Is.
Sta Cruz Is.
Espiritu Santo
Mallicolo
Loyalty Is.
New Caledonia
NICKEL
SANDALWOOD
COFFEE

P A C I F I C   O C E A N

Coral Sea

QUEENSLAND
Rockhampton
Townsville
Brisbane
Cooktown
Normanton
Forsyth
Charters Towers
Winton
Charleville
Quilpie

NORTH AUSTRALIA
CENTRAL AUSTRALIA
Arnhem Land
Gulf of Carpentaria
Darwin
Pine Creek
Alice Springs
Telegraph
Overland
Tanami

WESTERN AUSTRALIA
TIN
GOLD
JARRAH
Perth
Fremantle
Kalgoorlie
Coolgardie
Carnarvon
Geraldton
Broome
Derby
Wyndham
Halls Creek

SOUTH AUSTRALIA
Adelaide
Port Augusta
L. Eyre
L. Torrens
L. Gairdner
Kangaroo I.
Great Australian Bight
Nullarbor Plain
Eucla

NEW SOUTH WALES
Sydney
Newcastle
Broken Hill
Bourke
Bathurst
Wollongong
Parramatta
Canberra
Tamworth
Grafton

VICTORIA
Melbourne
Ballarat
Bendigo
Geelong

TASMANIA
Hobart
Launceston
Bass Str.
Tasman Sea

NEW ZEALAND
North I.
South I.
Auckland
Wellington
Christchurch
Dunedin
New Plymouth
Hokitika
Invercargill
Stewart I.
Chatham Is.
Norfolk I.
Lord Howe I.

I N D I A N   O C E A N

Tropic of Capricorn

NOTE TO COLOURING

Dairy Produce	
Cattle Breeding with Wool and Mutton	
Wool and Mutton	
Fisheries	

Other Products are named in Red
Navigable Rivers

Sugar
Copra
Pearls and Mother of Pearl
Gold

Scale 1:26,000,000
English Miles
Kilometres

Longitude East 140 of Greenwich

Bonne's Projection

The Edinburgh Geographical Institute
John Bartholomew & Son Ltd.

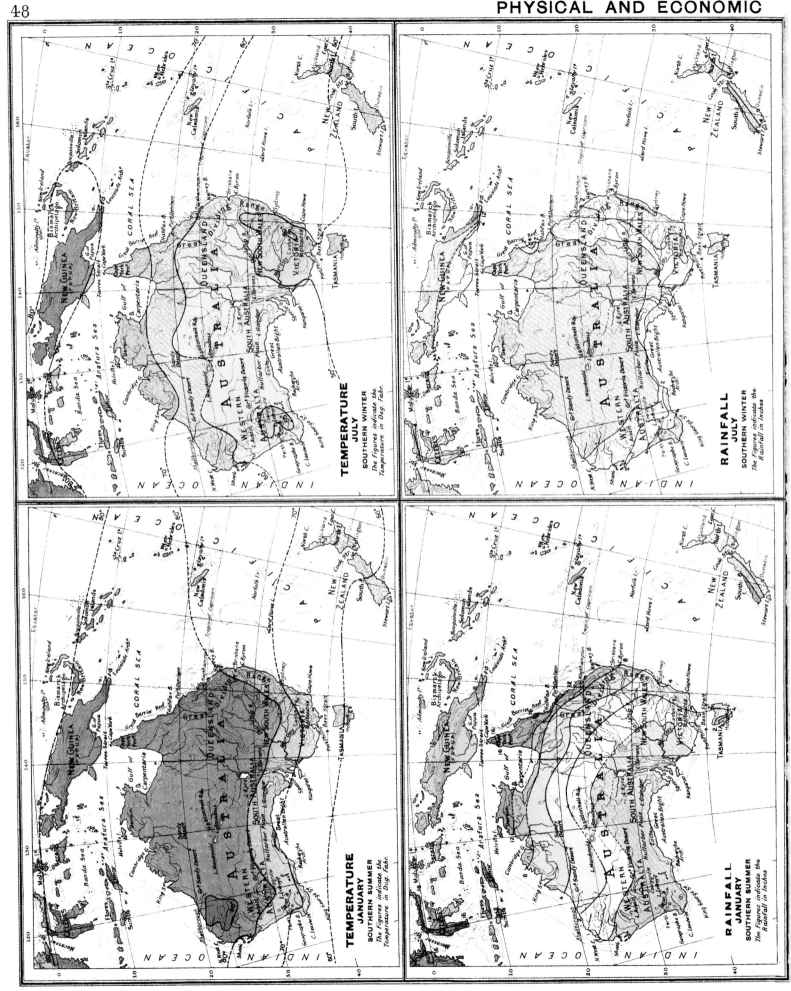

TEMPERATURE
JULY
SOUTHERN WINTER
The Figures indicate the
Temperature in Deg. Fahr.

RAINFALL
JULY
SOUTHERN WINTER
The Figures indicate the
Rainfall in Inches

TEMPERATURE
JANUARY
SOUTHERN SUMMER
The Figures indicate the
Temperature in Deg. Fahr.

RAINFALL
JANUARY
SOUTHERN SUMMER
The Figures indicate the
Rainfall in Inches

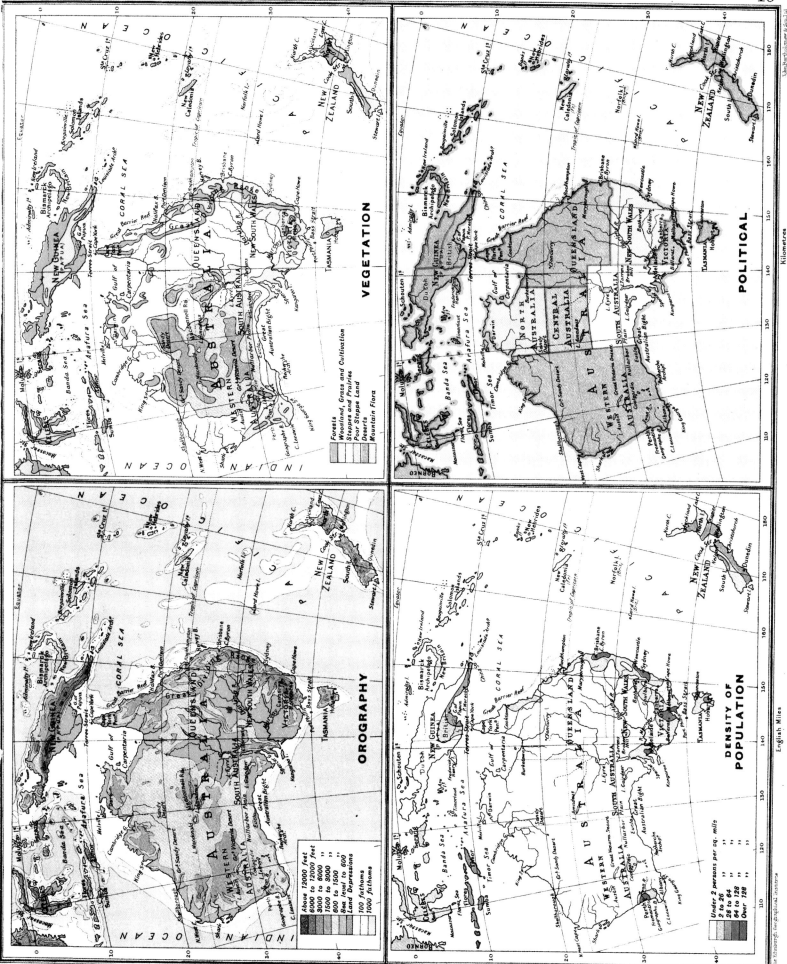

VEGETATION

Forests
Woodland, Grass and Cultivation
Steppes and Prairies
Poor Steppe Land
Deserts
Mountain Flora

POLITICAL

Kilometres

OROGRAPHY

Above 12000 feet
6000 to 12000 feet
3000 to 6000 "
1500 to 3000 "
600 to 1500 "
Sea level to 600 "
Land Depressions
100 fathoms
1000 fathoms

DENSITY OF POPULATION

Under 2 persons per sq. mile
2 to 26 " " "
26 to 64 " " "
64 to 128 " " "
Over 128 " " "

English Miles

SOUTH-EAST AUSTRALIA AND NEW ZEALAND

NORTH ISLAND

SOUTH ISLAND

SOUTH PACIFIC OCEAN

Scale 1:7,200,000
English Miles
Kilometres
Railways

Longitude East 172 of Greenwich

NOTE TO COLOURING

Coal · Silver · Kauri Gum
Live Stock · Wine · Gold
Other Products are named in Red

QUEENSLAND

NEW SOUTH WALES

SOUTH AUSTRALIA

VICTORIA

TASMANIA

INDIAN OCEAN

SYDNEY

HOBART

BASS STRAIT

Tropic of Capricorn

Scale 1:12,000,000
English Miles
Kilometres
Railways

Longitude East of Greenwich

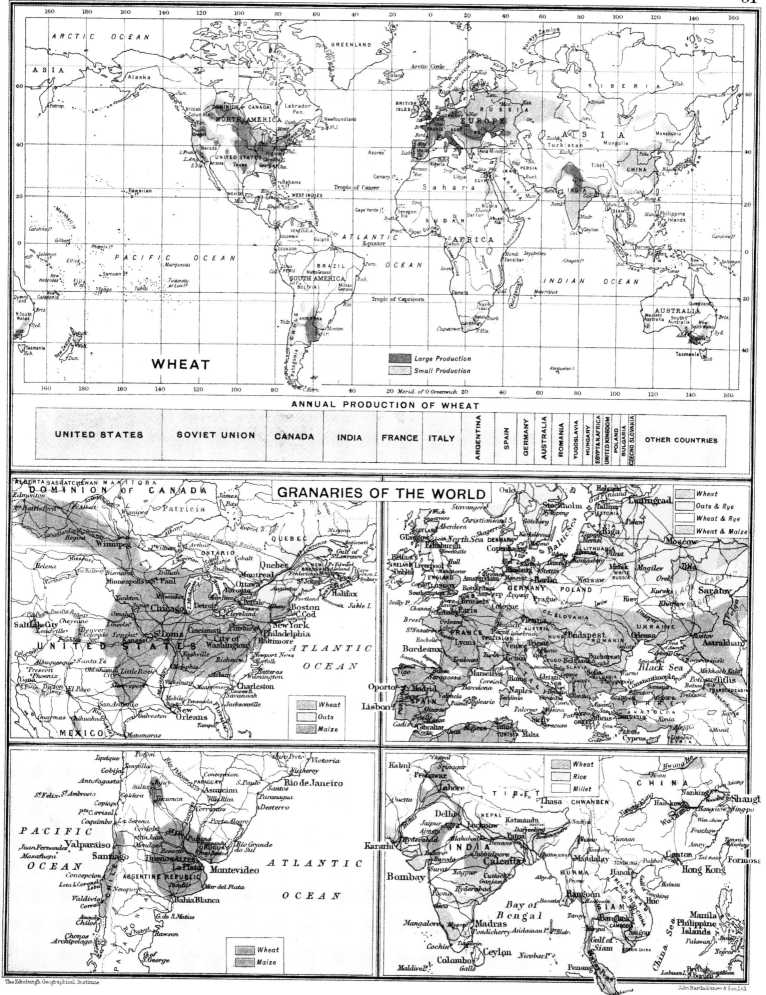

WHEAT

Large Production
Small Production

ANNUAL PRODUCTION OF WHEAT

UNITED STATES	SOVIET UNION	CANADA	INDIA	FRANCE	ITALY	ARGENTINA	SPAIN	GERMANY	AUSTRALIA	ROMANIA	YUGOSLAVIA	HUNGARY	EGYPT & AFRICA	UNITED KINGDOM	POLAND	BULGARIA	CZECHO SLOVAKIA	OTHER COUNTRIES

GRANARIES OF THE WORLD

Wheat
Oats & Rye
Wheat & Rye
Wheat & Maize

Wheat
Oats
Maize

Wheat
Maize

Wheat
Rice
Millet

The Edinburgh Geographical Institute

John Bartholomew & Son, Ltd.

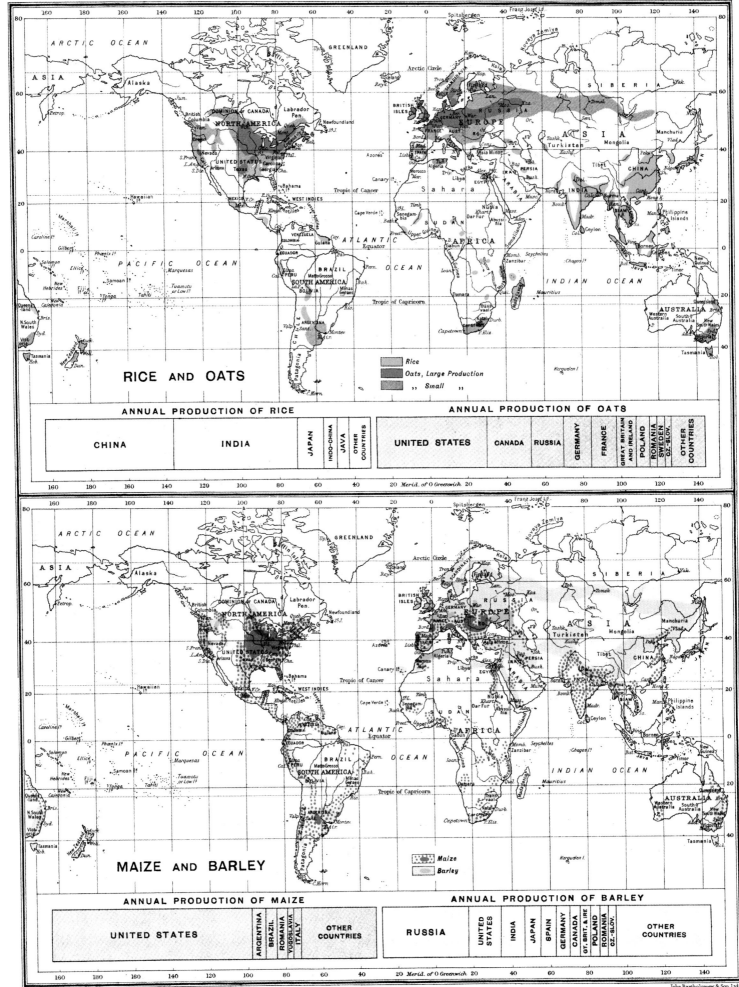

RICE AND OATS

	Rice
	Oats, Large Production
	„ Small „

ANNUAL PRODUCTION OF RICE

CHINA	INDIA	JAPAN	INDO-CHINA	JAVA	OTHER COUNTRIES

ANNUAL PRODUCTION OF OATS

UNITED STATES	CANADA	RUSSIA	GERMANY	FRANCE	GREAT BRITAIN AND IRELAND	POLAND	ROMANIA	SWEDEN	CZ.-SLOV.	OTHER COUNTRIES

MAIZE AND BARLEY

| | Maize |
| | Barley |

ANNUAL PRODUCTION OF MAIZE

UNITED STATES	ARGENTINA	BRAZIL	ROMANIA	YUGOSLAVIA	ITALY	OTHER COUNTRIES

ANNUAL PRODUCTION OF BARLEY

RUSSIA	UNITED STATES	INDIA	JAPAN	SPAIN	GERMANY	CANADA	GT. BRIT. & IRE.	POLAND	ROMANIA	CZ.-SLOV.	OTHER COUNTRIES

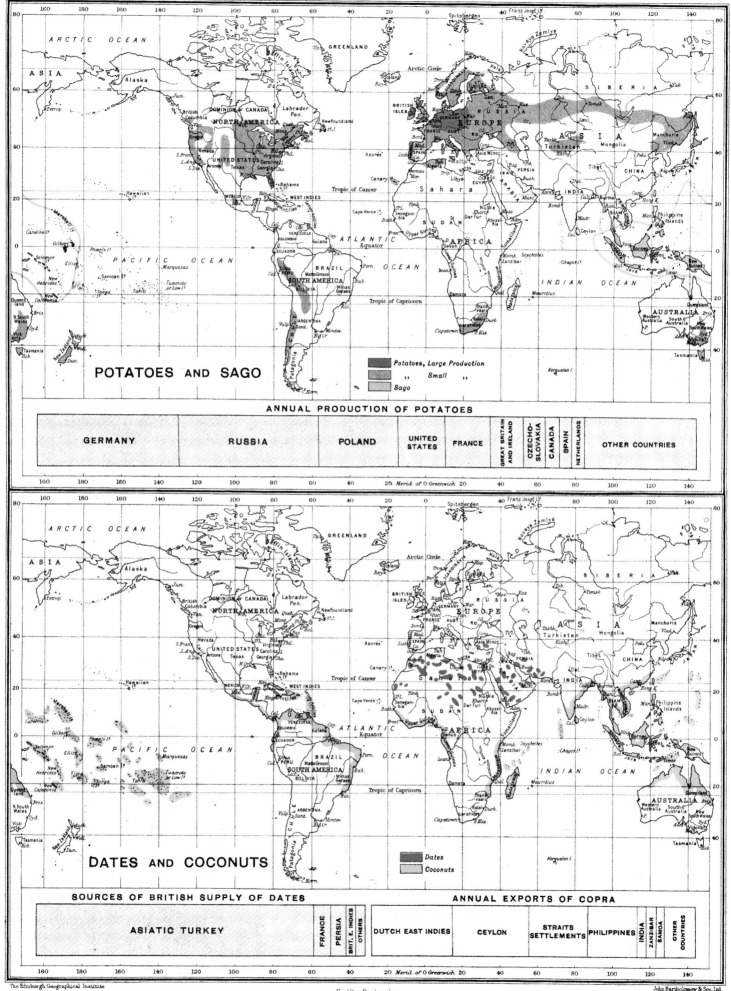

POTATOES AND SAGO

▨	Potatoes, Large Production
▨	„ Small „
▨	Sago

ANNUAL PRODUCTION OF POTATOES

GERMANY	RUSSIA	POLAND	UNITED STATES	FRANCE	GREAT BRITAIN AND IRELAND	CZECHO-SLOVAKIA	CANADA	SPAIN	NETHERLANDS	OTHER COUNTRIES

DATES AND COCONUTS

▨	Dates
▨	Coconuts

SOURCES OF BRITISH SUPPLY OF DATES

ASIATIC TURKEY	FRANCE	PERSIA	BRIT. E. INDIES	OTHERS

ANNUAL EXPORTS OF COPRA

DUTCH EAST INDIES	CEYLON	STRAITS SETTLEMENTS	PHILIPPINES	INDIA	ZANZIBAR	SAMOA	OTHER COUNTRIES

The Edinburgh Geographical Institute   Gall's Projection   John Bartholomew & Son, Ltd.

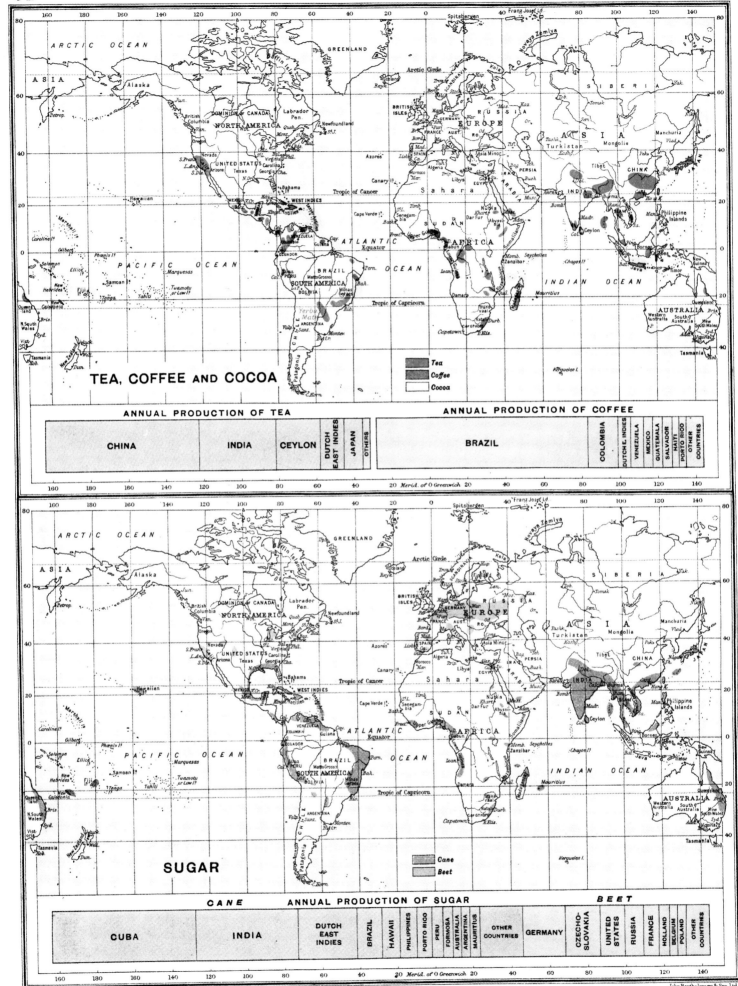

TEA, COFFEE AND COCOA

Tea
Coffee
Cocoa

ANNUAL PRODUCTION OF TEA

CHINA	INDIA	CEYLON	DUTCH EAST INDIES	JAPAN	OTHERS

ANNUAL PRODUCTION OF COFFEE

BRAZIL	COLOMBIA	DUTCH. INDIES	VENEZUELA	MEXICO	GUATEMALA	SALVADOR	HAITI	PORTO RICO	OTHER COUNTRIES

Merid. of 0 Greenwich

SUGAR

Cane
Beet

ANNUAL PRODUCTION OF SUGAR

CANE   *BEET*

CUBA	INDIA	DUTCH EAST INDIES	BRAZIL	HAWAII	PHILIPPINES	PORTO RICO	PERU	FORMOSA	AUSTRALIA	ARGENTINA	MAURITIUS	OTHER COUNTRIES	GERMANY	CZECHO-SLOVAKIA	UNITED STATES	RUSSIA	FRANCE	BELGIUM	POLAND	OTHER COUNTRIES

Merid. of 0 Greenwich

The Edinburgh Geographical Institute

Gall's Projection

John Bartholomew & Son, Ltd.

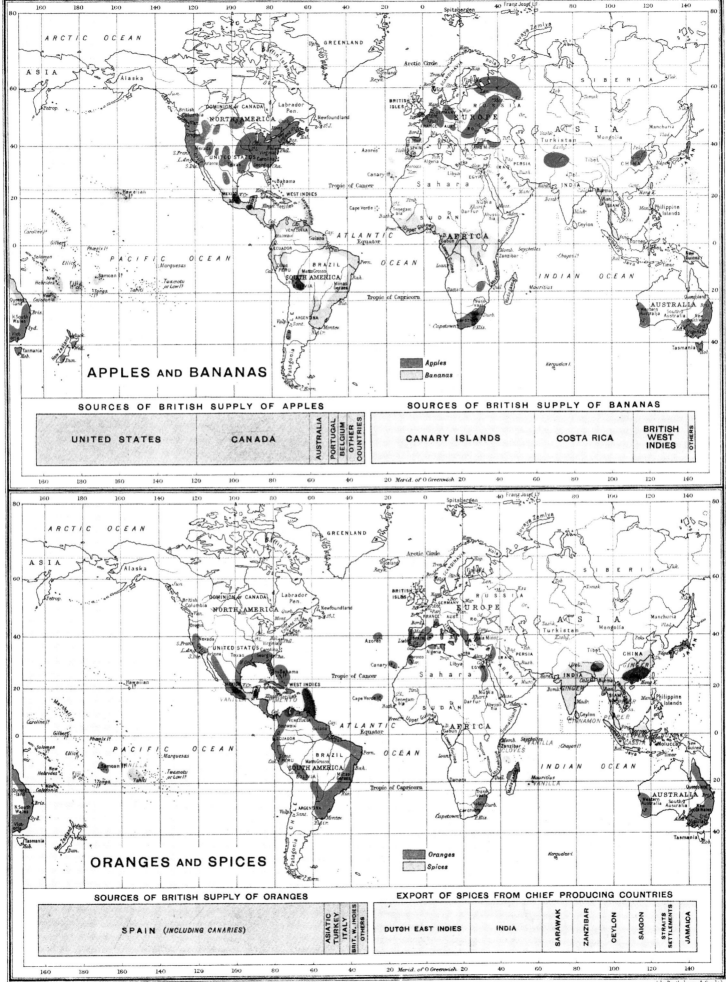

APPLES AND BANANAS

Apples
Bananas

SOURCES OF BRITISH SUPPLY OF APPLES					
UNITED STATES	CANADA	AUSTRALIA	PORTUGAL	BELGIUM	OTHER COUNTRIES

SOURCES OF BRITISH SUPPLY OF BANANAS			
CANARY ISLANDS	COSTA RICA	BRITISH WEST INDIES	OTHERS

ORANGES AND SPICES

Oranges
Spices

SOURCES OF BRITISH SUPPLY OF ORANGES				
SPAIN (INCLUDING CANARIES)	ASIATIC TURKEY	ITALY	BRIT. W. INDIES	OTHERS

EXPORT OF SPICES FROM CHIEF PRODUCING COUNTRIES							
DUTCH EAST INDIES	INDIA	SARAWAK	ZANZIBAR	CEYLON	SAIGON	STRAITS SETTLEMENTS	JAMAICA

The Edinburgh Geographical Institute

Gall's Projection

John Bartholomew & Son, Ltd.

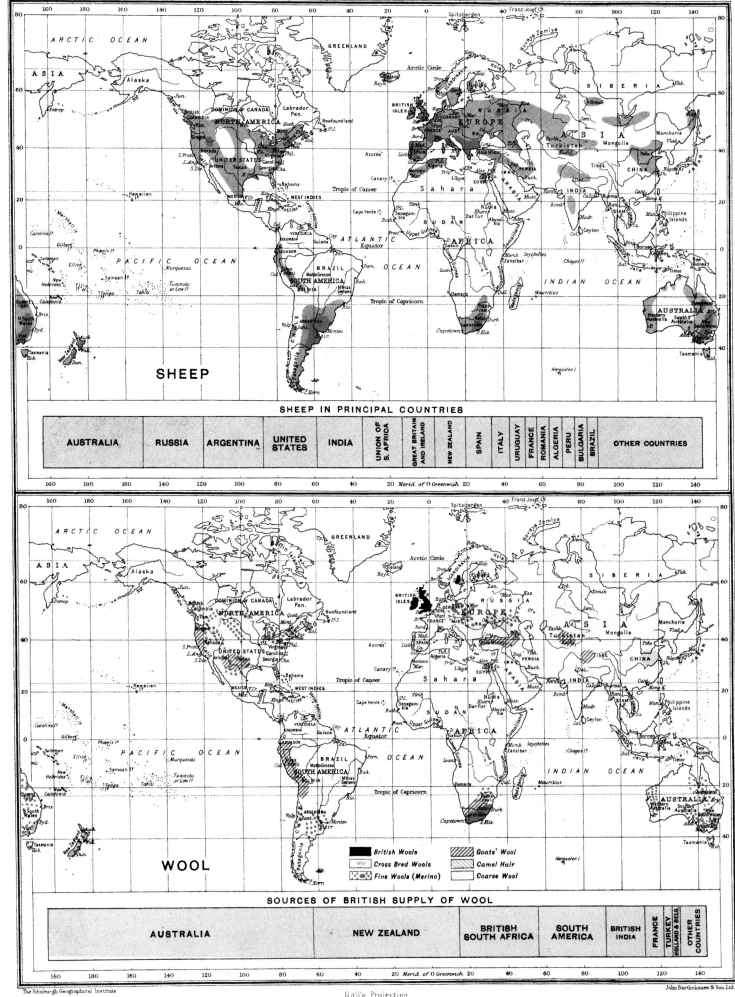

SHEEP

SHEEP IN PRINCIPAL COUNTRIES

| AUSTRALIA | RUSSIA | ARGENTINA | UNITED STATES | INDIA | UNION OF S. AFRICA | GREAT BRITAIN AND IRELAND | NEW ZEALAND | SPAIN | ITALY | URUGUAY | FRANCE | ROMANIA | ALGERIA | PERU | BULGARIA | BRAZIL | OTHER COUNTRIES |

WOOL

British Wools
Cross Bred Wools
Fine Wools (Merino)
Goats' Wool
Camel Hair
Coarse Wool

SOURCES OF BRITISH SUPPLY OF WOOL

| AUSTRALIA | NEW ZEALAND | BRITISH SOUTH AFRICA | SOUTH AMERICA | BRITISH INDIA | FRANCE | TURKEY | HOLLAND & BELG. | OTHER COUNTRIES |

The Edinburgh Geographical Institute

Gall's Projection

John Bartholomew & Son, Ltd.

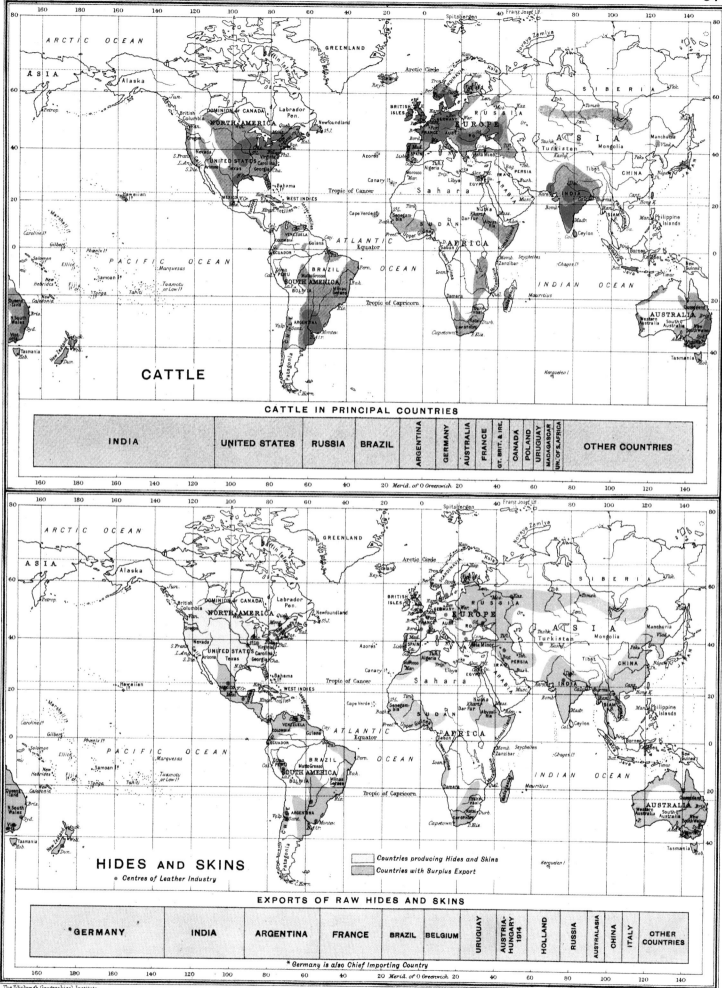

CATTLE

CATTLE IN PRINCIPAL COUNTRIES

INDIA	UNITED STATES	RUSSIA	BRAZIL	ARGENTINA	GERMANY	AUSTRALIA	FRANCE	GT. BRIT. & IRE.	CANADA	POLAND	URUGUAY	MADAGASCAR	UN. OF S.AFRICA	OTHER COUNTRIES

HIDES AND SKINS

• Centres of Leather Industry

Countries producing Hides and Skins

Countries with Surplus Export

EXPORTS OF RAW HIDES AND SKINS

*GERMANY	INDIA	ARGENTINA	FRANCE	BRAZIL	BELGIUM	URUGUAY	AUSTRIA-HUNGARY 1914	HOLLAND	RUSSIA	AUSTRALASIA	CHINA	ITALY	OTHER COUNTRIES

*Germany is also Chief Importing Country

The Edinburgh Geographical Institute

Gall's Projection

John Bartholomew & Son. Ltd.

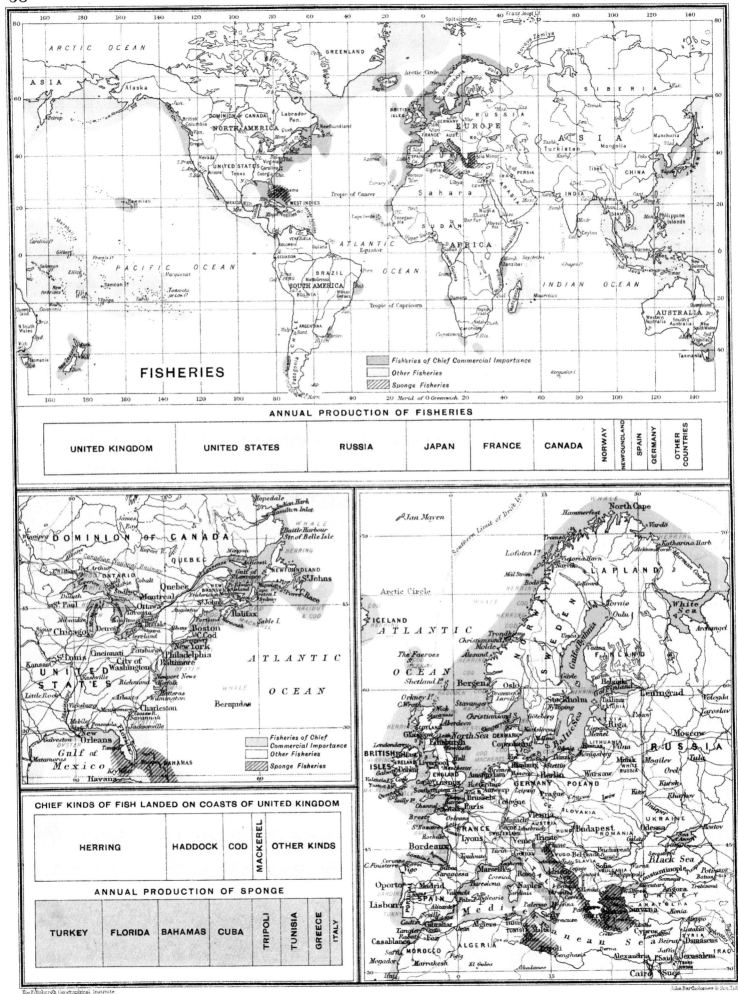

FISHERIES

Fisheries of Chief Commercial Importance
Other Fisheries
Sponge Fisheries

ANNUAL PRODUCTION OF FISHERIES

UNITED KINGDOM	UNITED STATES	RUSSIA	JAPAN	FRANCE	CANADA	NORWAY	NEWFOUNDLAND	SPAIN	GERMANY	OTHER COUNTRIES

Fisheries of Chief Commercial Importance
Other Fisheries
Sponge Fisheries

CHIEF KINDS OF FISH LANDED ON COASTS OF UNITED KINGDOM

HERRING	HADDOCK	COD	MACKEREL	OTHER KINDS

ANNUAL PRODUCTION OF SPONGE

TURKEY	FLORIDA	BAHAMAS	CUBA	TRIPOLI	TUNISIA	GREECE	ITALY

The Edinburgh Geographical Institute

John Bartholomew & Son Ltd.

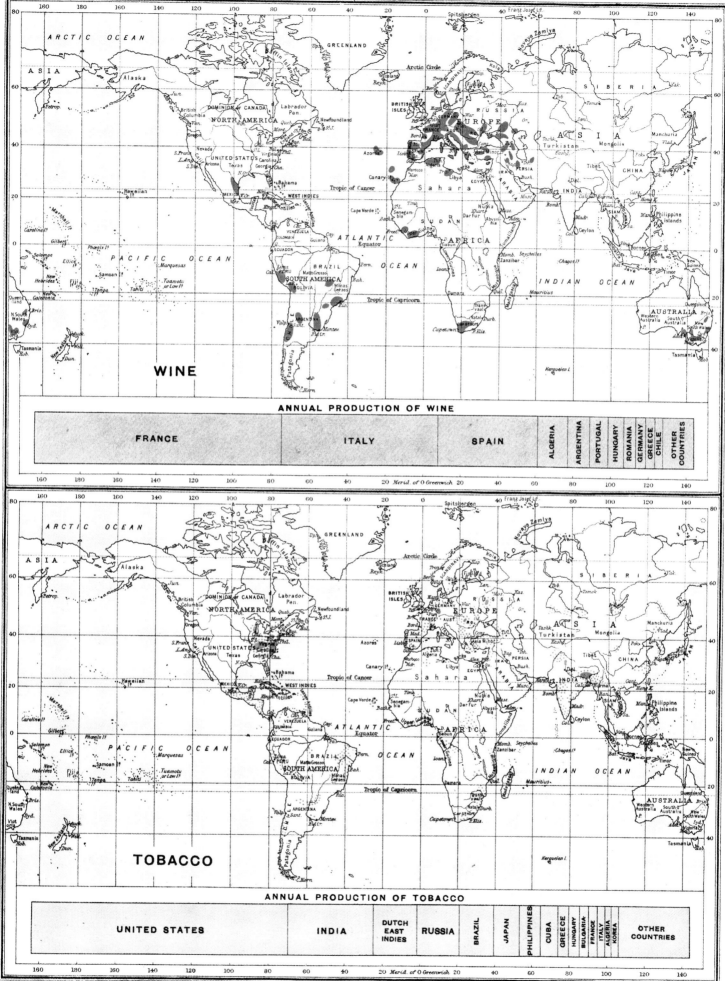

WINE

ANNUAL PRODUCTION OF WINE

FRANCE	ITALY	SPAIN	ALGERIA	ARGENTINA	PORTUGAL	HUNGARY	ROMANIA	GERMANY	GREECE	CHILE	OTHER COUNTRIES

TOBACCO

ANNUAL PRODUCTION OF TOBACCO

UNITED STATES	INDIA	DUTCH EAST INDIES	RUSSIA	BRAZIL	JAPAN	PHILIPPINES	CUBA	GREECE	HUNGARY	BULGARIA	FRANCE	ITALY	ALGERIA	KOREA	OTHER COUNTRIES

Gall's Projection

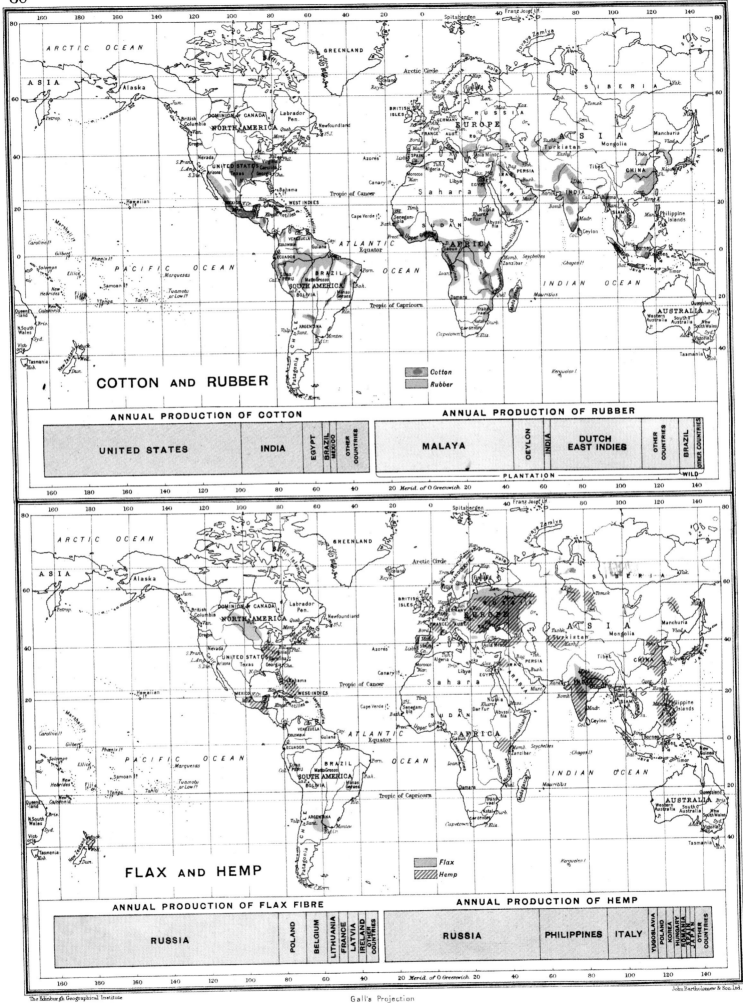

COTTON AND RUBBER

Cotton
Rubber

ANNUAL PRODUCTION OF COTTON						ANNUAL PRODUCTION OF RUBBER						
UNITED STATES	INDIA	EGYPT	MEXICO	BRAZIL	OTHER COUNTRIES	MALAYA	CEYLON	INDIA	DUTCH EAST INDIES	OTHER COUNTRIES	BRAZIL	OTHER COUNTRIES

PLANTATION — WILD

FLAX AND HEMP

Flax
Hemp

ANNUAL PRODUCTION OF FLAX FIBRE								ANNUAL PRODUCTION OF HEMP								
RUSSIA	POLAND	BELGIUM	LITHUANIA	FRANCE	LATVIA	IRELAND	OTHER COUNTRIES	RUSSIA	PHILIPPINES	ITALY	YUGOSLAVIA	POLAND	KOREA	HUNGARY	RUMANIA	SPAIN	JAPAN	OTHER COUNTRIES

The Edinburgh Geographical Institute

Gall's Projection

John Bartholomew & Son, Ltd.

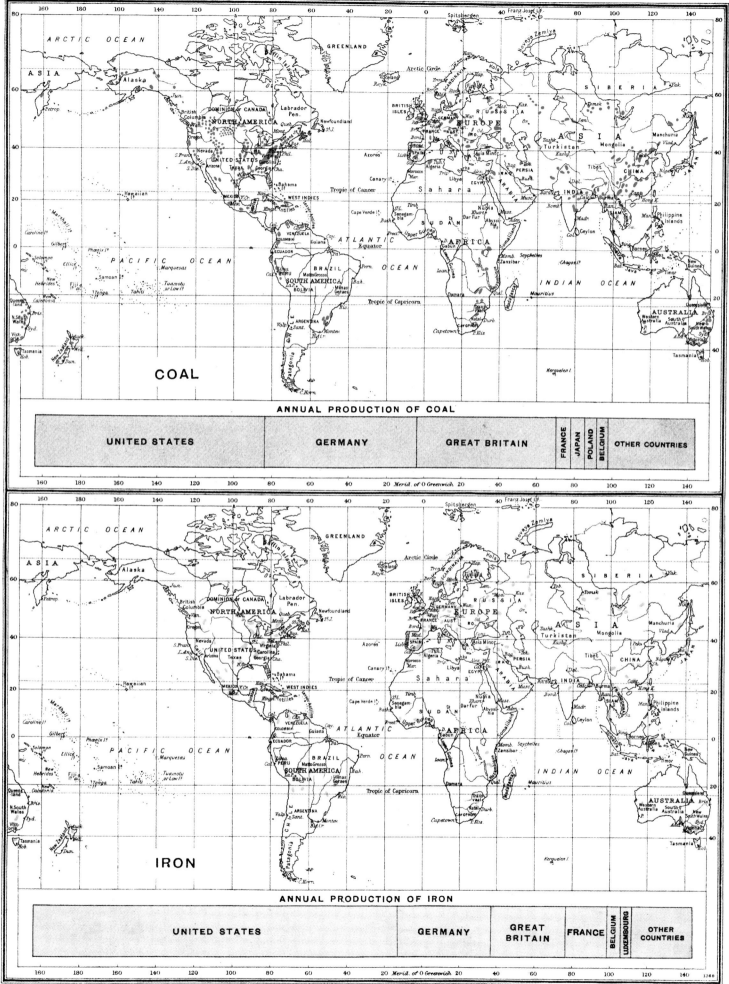

COAL

ANNUAL PRODUCTION OF COAL

UNITED STATES	GERMANY	GREAT BRITAIN	FRANCE	JAPAN	POLAND	BELGIUM	OTHER COUNTRIES

IRON

ANNUAL PRODUCTION OF IRON

UNITED STATES	GERMANY	GREAT BRITAIN	FRANCE	BELGIUM	LUXEMBOURG	OTHER COUNTRIES

The Edinburgh Geographical Institute

Gall's Projection

John Bartholomew & Son, Ltd.

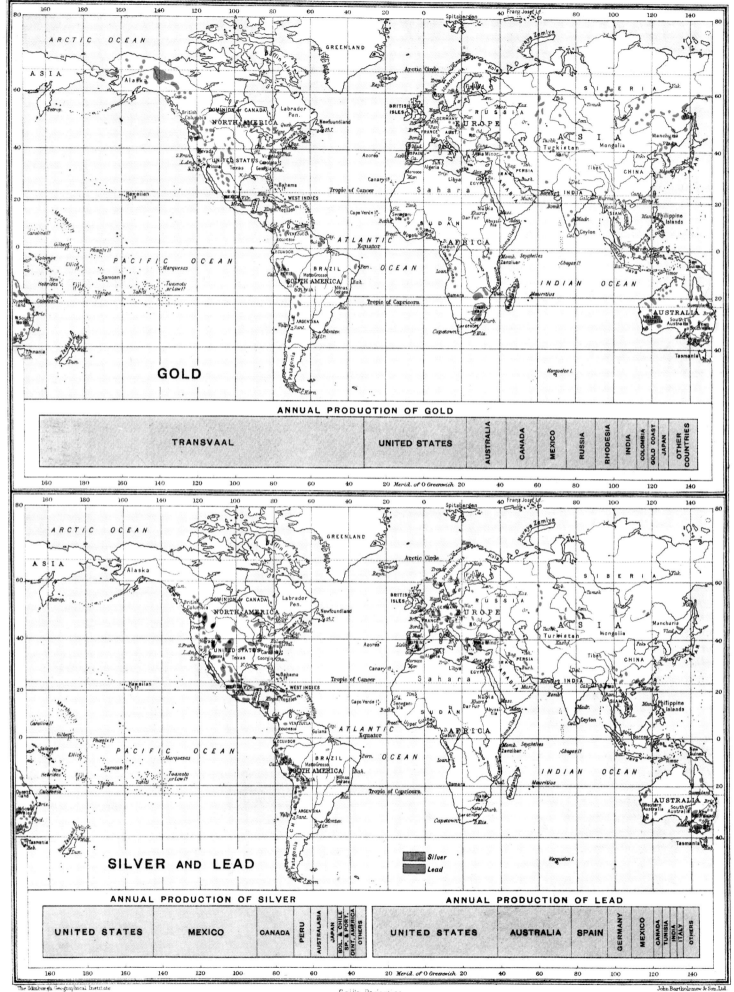

GOLD

ANNUAL PRODUCTION OF GOLD

TRANSVAAL		UNITED STATES	AUSTRALIA	CANADA	MEXICO	RUSSIA	RHODESIA	INDIA	COLOMBIA	GOLD COAST	JAPAN	OTHER COUNTRIES

SILVER AND LEAD

Silver
Lead

ANNUAL PRODUCTION OF SILVER

UNITED STATES	MEXICO	CANADA	PERU	AUSTRALASIA	JAPAN	BOL. & CHILE SP. & PORT. CENT. AMERICA	OTHERS

ANNUAL PRODUCTION OF LEAD

UNITED STATES	AUSTRALIA	SPAIN	GERMANY	MEXICO	CANADA TUNISIA INDIA ITALY	OTHERS

The Edinburgh Geographical Institute.   Gall's Projection   John Bartholomew & Son, Ltd.

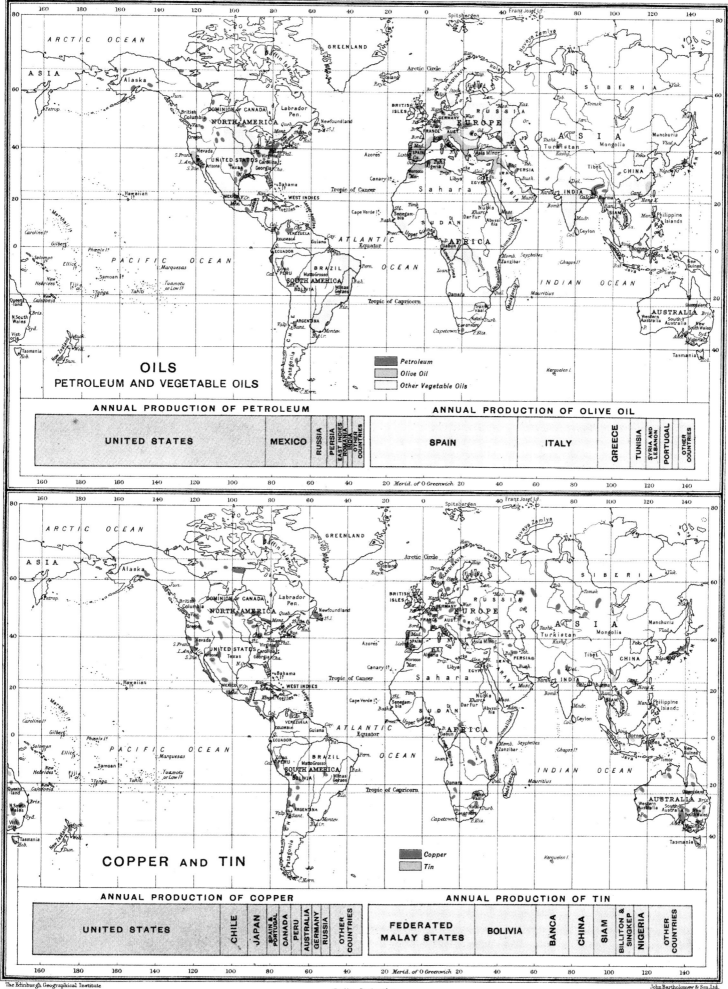

OILS
PETROLEUM AND VEGETABLE OILS

- Petroleum
- Olive Oil
- Other Vegetable Oils

ANNUAL PRODUCTION OF PETROLEUM							ANNUAL PRODUCTION OF OLIVE OIL					
UNITED STATES	MEXICO	RUSSIA	PERSIA	EAST INDIES	ROMANIA	OTHER COUNTRIES	SPAIN	ITALY	GREECE	TUNISIA	SYRIA AND LEBANON	PORTUGAL	OTHER COUNTRIES

COPPER AND TIN

- Copper
- Tin

ANNUAL PRODUCTION OF COPPER									ANNUAL PRODUCTION OF TIN					
UNITED STATES	CHILE	JAPAN	SPAIN & PORTUGAL	CANADA	PERU	AUSTRALIA	GERMANY	RUSSIA	OTHER COUNTRIES	FEDERATED MALAY STATES	BOLIVIA	BANCA	CHINA	SIAM	BILLITON & SINGKEP	NIGERIA	OTHER COUNTRIES

The Edinburgh Geographical Institute

Gall's Projection

John Bartholomew & Son, Ltd.

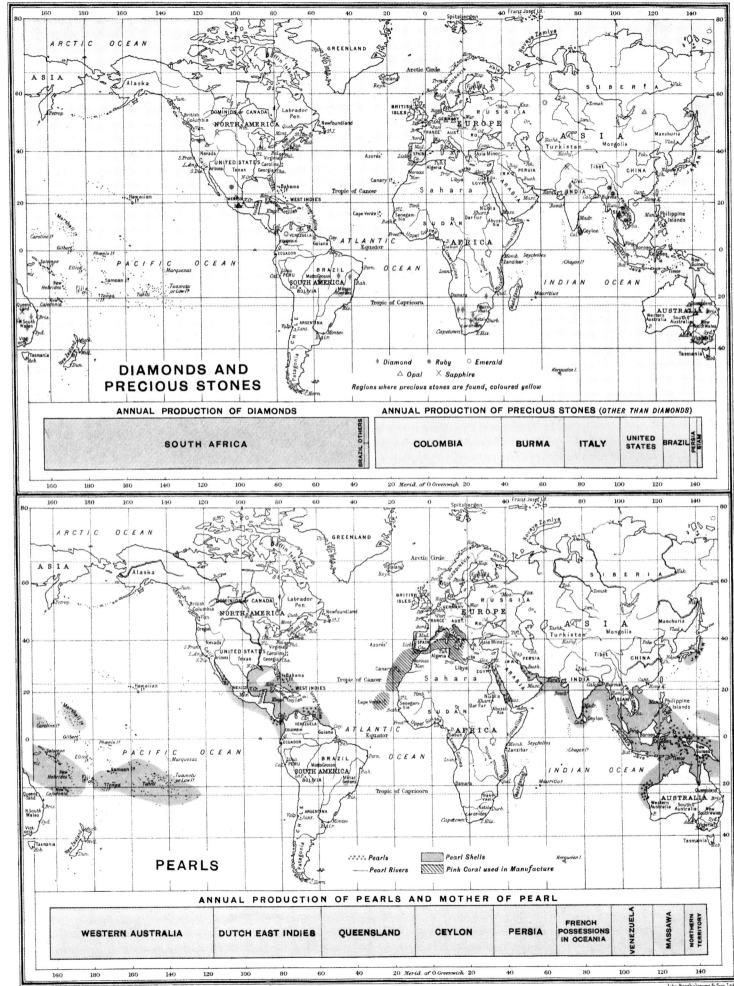

DIAMONDS AND PRECIOUS STONES

◆ Diamond ● Ruby ○ Emerald
△ Opal ✕ Sapphire

Regions where precious stones are found, coloured yellow

ANNUAL PRODUCTION OF DIAMONDS		ANNUAL PRODUCTION OF PRECIOUS STONES (*OTHER THAN DIAMONDS*)					
SOUTH AFRICA	BRAZIL OTHERS	COLOMBIA	BURMA	ITALY	UNITED STATES	BRAZIL	PERSIA SIAM

PEARLS

⋯ Pearls   Pearl Shells
— Pearl Rivers   Pink Coral used in Manufacture

ANNUAL PRODUCTION OF PEARLS AND MOTHER OF PEARL								
WESTERN AUSTRALIA	DUTCH EAST INDIES	QUEENSLAND	CEYLON	PERSIA	FRENCH POSSESSIONS IN OCEANIA	VENEZUELA	MASSAWA	NORTHERN TERRITORY

Merid. of 0 Greenwich

Gall's Projection

The Edinburgh Geographical Institute

John Bartholomew & Son,Ltd.